The French Historical Narrative and the Fall of France

The French Historical Narrative and the Fall of France

Simone Weil and Her Contemporaries Face the Debacle

Christine Ann Evans

LEXINGTON BOOKS
Lanham • Boulder • New York • London

Published by Lexington Books
An imprint of The Rowman & Littlefield Publishing Group, Inc.
4501 Forbes Boulevard, Suite 200, Lanham, Maryland 20706
www.rowman.com

86-90 Paul Street, London EC2A 4NE

Copyright © 2022 by The Rowman & Littlefield Publishing Group, Inc.

All rights reserved. No part of this book may be reproduced in any form or by any electronic or mechanical means, including information storage and retrieval systems, without written permission from the publisher, except by a reviewer who may quote passages in a review.

British Library Cataloguing in Publication Information Available

Library of Congress Cataloging-in-Publication Data

Names: Evans, Christine Ann, author.
Title: The French historical narrative and the fall of France : Simone Weil and her contemporaries face the debacle / Christine Ann Evans.
Other titles: Simone Weil and her contemporaries face the debacle
Description: Lanham : Lexington Books, [2022] | Includes bibliographical references and index.
Identifiers: LCCN 2022021705 (print) | LCCN 2022021706 (ebook) | ISBN 9781793646668 (cloth) | ISBN 9781793646682 (paperback) | ISBN 9781793646675 (ebook)
Subjects: LCSH: France—History—Third Republic, 1870-1940—Historiography. | World War, 1939-1945—France—Influence. | Weil, Simone, 1909-1943. Enracinement. | Weil, Simone, 1909-1943—Social and political views. | France—Intellectual life—20th century—Historiography. | Collective memory—France. | Nationalism—France. | Group identity—France—History. | France—History—German occupation, 1940-1945—Social aspects.
Classification: LCC DC335 .E93 2022 (print) | LCC DC335 (ebook) | DDC 944.081/6—dc23/eng/20220622
LC record available at https://lccn.loc.gov/2022021705
LC ebook record available at https://lccn.loc.gov/2022021706

Contents

Preface — vii

1 Historical Narrative and the Founding of the French Third Republic — 1

2 The Double Challenge to "Sacred History": Interwar Pacifism and the 150th Commemoration of the French Revolution in 1939 — 27

3 The Debacle: The Debate Engaged — 55

In the Way of a Conclusion — 87

Bibliography — 105

Index — 115

About the Author — 121

Preface

The French Third Republic fell to the Nazi forces on June 25, 1940, after a scant three weeks of armed combat. Paris was declared an open city on June 10, and some six million Frenchmen and women took to the roads as refugees to get out of the path of the advancing German forces. The defeat was such a thoroughgoing calamity that the French termed it "the Debacle." How, they wondered, could a country whose democratic ideals and government served as a beacon for the rest of the world have crumbled so utterly and so quickly in the face of Fascist forces? The French will attempt to arrive at an adequate response to this question during the war years and those immediately following.

The post-Debacle debate will engage many prominent figures, some of whom are recognizable to a global audience (Léon Blum and Charles De Gaulle), others who have since fallen into relative obscurity (Robert Brasillach). These voices represent the range of political views held at the time, but no matter how far distant on the political spectrum, they all share a frame of reference that serves as a point of departure for their analyses: France's "sacred history" as constructed and espoused by the Third Republic. This "official history" enshrined the French Revolution as a great leap forward in world history and the foundational event for modern France; celebrated France's role in spreading the concepts of human rights beyond her borders; associated progress with the concerted campaign to turn "peasants into Frenchman," in Eugen Weber's words, to form a modern national comity to replace more traditional and local roots. To ponder French history during wartime occupation constituted no mere academic exercise. In Anne-Marie Thiesse's formulation, "When the future has broken down, the conflicts to determine the past become radicalized."[1] To understand the disaster facing them and to imagine a future, the French had to interrogate the past that had forged them into a people with a specific identity with shared (albeit contested) values.

This study begins with the construction of France's sacred history in the years following the founding of the Third Republic in 1871; it will then move to the years 1938–1945, at times straying beyond those dates. The wartime debate on France's history did not launch after 1940; it had been queued up and primed beforehand. September of 1938 marks a significant moment: France and her Allies signed the Munich Agreement, the apogee of appeasement of Nazi Germany. The relief France felt at the conclusion of that accord was counterbalanced by dread. All the signatory countries realized the agreement was the last waystation before a momentous conflict, and while celebrating a reprieve, all girded their loins for war. And the debate on French history did not end with the defeat of Nazi Germany. The year 1945 marks the end of the war, of course, and also saw the trials of Vichy's major political figures for collaboration. These inquiries were intended to arrive at the root causes of the Debacle, to punish those responsible and thus to draw a line after wartime, to "get beyond it" in a summary fashion. But the specters of the past were not so easily laid.

Simone Weil's analyses will serve as the heart of this study. As both an actor in much of what occurred during that period and one of its most astute commentators, hers is a privileged and valuable viewpoint.[2] She was deeply engaged at various times of her life in trade unionism, the pacifist movement, education, and the efforts of *la France combattante*, De Gaulle's group in London. She also, though, remained alert to all the aporias in these various organizations and systems. Trained as a philosopher, she made important contributions to that field as well as to the fields of political thought, theology and, as I hope to demonstrate, history. As one of the most accomplished products of the French educational system, she represented that world but at the same time remained a stubborn outsider who believed her insights could best inform from an outlier position.

Weil was born in Paris in 1909 into a cultivated Jewish family with origins in Russia and Alsace.[3] Her father, Bernard, was a doctor, her mother, Selma, an intelligent woman whose efforts were focused on her two bright children, Simone and André. The older brother showed early on the precocious gift for mathematics that was crowned by a career at the Institute for Advanced Study and the award of the Kyoto Prize, one of the most prestigious recognitions in the field of mathematics.

Weil's schooling was that reserved for the most gifted and privileged of French students: at the Lycée Henri IV, she studied with the philosopher and public intellectual Alain; she entered the *École Normale Supérieure*, the *Grande École* or competitive exam school that trained students to join the professoriate and quite often saw them take leadership positions in French society (the philosophers Jean-Paul Sartre and Maurice Merleau-Ponty were students while she was there; the politicians and eventually French prime ministers Jean Jaurès and Léon Blum had preceded her as students). She passed the *agrégation* exam in philosophy, the crown of French academic achievement. Her schooling represented the gold standard of the very competitive, rigorous French educational system.

The career path of most of her fellow *normaliens* and *agrégés* would begin with teaching at the more desirable *lycées* or classical high schools (i.e., those closer to Paris in larger towns), hoping eventually to land in a position in Paris (as did Sartre), and eventually moving into university teaching or other more prestigious government service. Weil chose to live against this careerist current; she requested postings to industrial cities where she could engage with the working class and further trade unionism (Le Puy, Auxerre, and Roanne). Her enduring conviction that work was central to human experience and her desire to know first-hand the conditions endured by the greater number led her to take a leave of absence from teaching to work for several months in factories, and she intermittently did farm work. She was convinced that she needed, in order to write knowledgeably about work, to experience it from the inside rather than standing outside and making "inquiries."

When Paris was declared an open city with the advance of Nazi troops in 1940, the Weils were among the many who joined the mass exodus out of Paris toward the unoccupied south. The collaborationist Vichy regime passed Jewish Statutes in 1940 and 1941, one of which banned Jews from the professions, including teaching and medicine. The Weils, mother, father, and Simone felt impelled to leave France for the United States in 1942 (her brother had preceded them there). Simone took this step very reluctantly. From the moment she arrived in New York City, she sought ways of getting back to France to join the armed resistance against the Nazis; finding that impossible, she called on friends from the *École Normale Supérieure* to pull strings to bring her to London. There she took a position as a researcher on the *Comité Général d'Études* (CGE) or General Committee for Studies, a branch of De Gaulle's *la France combattante*. This group addressed a series of issues that would face the provisional government after the war, from how to carry out the trials against collaborators to what kind of constitution should replace that of the Third Republic. These projects spurred one of the most significant works of Weil's career: *L'Enracinement* or *The Need for Roots*. In this treatise, which will be the focus of the third chapter, she first sets out the needs of all human beings and argues that those needs have NOT, for the most part, been acknowledged and met in the French polity. She lays out the foundations for a newly imagined community that could meet the needs of France's soul. The narrative of French history is a prime focus throughout.

Exhaustion, heartbreak at her exile, and helpless compassion for what her compatriots were enduring contributed to her death due to tuberculosis in 1943.

Though an infinitely gifted and productive intellectual, Weil was no careerist, as stated previously. She wrote voluminously and constantly during her lifetime, two book-length manuscripts—*Réflexions sur les causes de la liberté et de l'oppression sociale* (1934) (*Oppression and Liberty*) and *The Need for Roots* (1943)—as well as articles, short and long, relatively little of which was published during her lifetime. Her family and friends gathered and edited her manuscripts for publication, and once her work came to the public's attention with the imprimatur of such figures as Albert Camus, T. S. Eliot, and Iris Murdoch, the significance of her thought was recognized more generally.

What follows is a brief outline of the "stages" of her thought and the major works which inform my focus. What I hope to trace is the continuity through these various stages; one is not "left behind" but persists in the next and following, all converging in her summa, *The Need for Roots*.

In the mid-1930s Weil was active in union work and organizing. As a member of the CGT, *Conféderation générale du travail* (General Confederation of Labor), a leftist union that espoused the dismantling of the class system, she wrote extensively on unionism, politics, Marxism, and revolt in publications with a specific editorial stance and readership, *La Révolution prolétarienne: L'École émancipée* (*The Proletarian Revolution: The Emancipated School*), among others. Despite her adherence to the CGT, she came to take a critical stance toward Marxist tenets, at least as an explanatory model for the enduring structures of society. In "Allons-nous vers une révolution prolétarienne?" ("Are We Headed for a Proletarian Revolution?"), she concludes that the Marxist model, even in the apotheosis of the worker state, could not free a worker from the monotony and passivity of being tied to the rhythms of a machine and a factory, and even if it were successful at dismantling economic structures, it had no proposals for tackling the social inequality created by the chasm separating "those who coordinate" and "those who execute."[4] In addition, the number of examples of any "worker state" are few—the Paris Commune in 1871 and the Russian Revolution in the years 1917 and 1918— both short-lived experiments. What grows out of the Russian state is an enormous "military and bureaucratic machine,"[5] not the hoped-for workers' state. And as difficult as this fact was for many of her comrades to face, as she reminds her reader, "Marx isn't dearer to us than truth."[6]

As the war approaches in the late 1930s, Weil turns her attention to it. In several articles written before the Munich Agreement of 1939, she argues for an integral pacifism and supports the French government's appeasement of Hitler. She abandons pacifism after the war is declared in 1939 and lays out her changed ideas on war and patriotism in "Réflexions en vue d'un bilan" ("Reflections in View of an Assessment"). Shortly after this article, she begins a line of inquiry that will engage her until the end of her life—the historical narrative constructed and embraced by the west that takes Rome as its starting point. This project begins in late 1939 with "Quelques réflexions sur les origines de l'hitlérisme" ("The Great Beast: Reflections on the Origins of Hitlerism"). Rome, she argues, rather than having been a civilizing influence, the hub and force for the unification of far-flung regions into a whole, instead "made a desert and called it peace," in words Tacitus attributes to a Breton chief.[7] Rome is the birthplace of Western society's original sin: it valorized conquest, centralization, and erasing of cultures—and equated all that with progress. These works will be discussed at greater length in chapter 2.

After she arrives in Marseille in 1940, she becomes a regular contributor to the *Cahiers du Sud*, a review that celebrated the cultural and historical community formed around the Mediterranean Sea. She appropriately published the article "L'Iliade, ou le poème de la force" ("The Iliad, or the Poem of Force") in that journal, as well as two articles dedicated to Occitanian culture, eradicated in the thirteenth century by marauding Northern French Crusaders and the Inquisition they brought with them. The focus of these three articles is of a piece with her writing on the "Origins of Hitlerism"—all explore the effects of force, whose nature is to exert itself to its fullest capacity, even to the point of eradicating rich cultures (Occitania and Troy). That such total annihilation is possible raises the specter of destruction for France.

Her time in Marseille was rich for another reason as well. Through Catholic friends, she met Father Marie-Joseph Perrin, a Dominican priest. Their frequent and long exchanges (not always comfortable) allowed her to more clearly formulate her newly forming intuitions on spirituality and faith. In a letter she would later write to the priest, she shares that her "conception of life" had been Christian since her earliest age, in her practice of a "poverty" and "purity" of spirit, her acceptance of God's will as a kind of *amor fati*, her love for her neighbor.[8] And once she had had a direct experience of Christ, when He came down and "seized" her.[9] She explores these spiritual questions in a series of essays as well as in her notebooks of the period, notebooks which she entrusted to Father Perrin and Gustave Thibon, a writer active in Catholic circles, when she left for the United States.

Thibon lovingly edited and organized the passages on spirituality and published them in a volume titled *La Pesanteur et la grâce* (*Gravity and Grace*). She uses the metaphor of gravity to suggest the entropic energy weighing humans down, with God's grace as the force that descends light-years of distance to draw human creatures out of gravity's strong pull. A key piece serves as a pivot between her spiritual and historical-political writings during this period, "La personne et le sacré" ("Human Personality"), where she identifies that core of the human being—not the "person," not what most would associate with a human personality, but the impersonal core of sacredness, which all future social and political systems must be structured to acknowledge and honor. If the concept of "rights" can be associated with the human person and revendication, it is "justice" alone that draws from the sacred. Weil comes back more than once to the incident of a criminal trial she witnessed: the accused was unable to express himself in any way that would have a positive impact on the verdict, while the judge enjoyed turning an elegant phrase. True attention was lacking in this case, on the part of the judge as well as the spectators, which meant true justice was absent. "Because affliction and truth need to be heard with the same attention, the spirit of justice and the spirit of truth are one."[10] Attention, as well as justice and obligations, will have to be the warp and woof of any new social structure.

Before she departed for New York, she wrote and left with Father Perrin the essay "L'Amour de Dieu et le malheur" ("The Love of God and Affliction"). Affliction is a suffering far beyond pain, so utter that it can "pulverize"[11] a person and deprive them of all that they associate with their self, reduce them in the eyes of the world to a figure of revulsion and horror, for loss of social recognition is inherent in affliction. It is a lesson for those with eyes to see that we are all mere "squatters" in our self-possession. But for Weil, affliction has a double edge—it can so purge all we cling to as part of our "I" that we are left empty, a space into which the recognition of the necessity of the world, grace, God have space to enter. In Weil's devastating simile of a nail that penetrates a being after a hammer blow, "The infinite distance which separates God and his creature gathers itself completely in a point to pierce a soul at its center."[12] But she is adamant that affliction is not God's "pedagogy" and that it is the worst of sins to push another into affliction, which "kills souls."[13] As Iris Murdoch has one of her characters ponder in *The Nice and Good*, "The kind of suffering that brings wisdom cannot be named and cannot without blasphemy be prayed for."[14] Understandably at that moment in 1942, she reflects on a specific population when she considers affliction—innocents "killed, tortured, driven out of their country, reduced to poverty or slavery, confined in camps or cells"[15]—those whom wartime has uprooted. Robert Chenavier reminds us that just as force can "pulverize" a single person, it can do the same to entire comity, and this is the specter Weil is contemplating.[16]

Again, these do not represent discontinuous "stages" in Weil's work; she does not separate from one in order to dedicate herself to the next; each one is brought forward to inform and enrich the following one. In her summa, *The Need for Roots*, she sets out the parameters for ensuring the worker exists not merely as a cog in an infernal machine; she posits the foundations for a hierarchy of responsibilities and obligations that does not crush those who are below and corrupt those at the top; she lays out the need for structures that recognize the "soul" of a country and of each of its members; she speculates on how to ensure the richness and robustness of the *milieu vital*, the vital medium from which souls take their nourishment and which has to be preserved to feed what is sacred in a person.

The above account of her work does not pretend to be exhaustive—it represents instead an idiosyncratic itinerary through Weil's writings, appropriate to the focus of this study. Other Weilians plot out alternative paths. And what follows does not aim to treat the entire range of her thought and contributions—philosophers, theologians, and political scientists have responded to her work from the expertise of their various disciplines.

Like many English-speaking Weilians, I came to Weil through Iris Murdoch. Murdoch spoke with high admiration of Weil and acknowledged what she owed to her, in particular, the concept of "attention" as a moral act that aspires to perceive the other or a situation as it is rather than through the fog of the "rat-runs of selfish daydream." Such praise from a writer I much admire brought me to Weil's *La Pesanteur et la grâce* (*Gravity and Grace*). Its short passages and aphorisms, a marvel of crystalline insight, expression, and impact, were garnered from her notebooks and organized into chapters by Gustave Thibon. I felt the wish to engage with Weil's thought. I brought to my study of her my background in literary studies and, in particular, narrative theory. She has been a constant, enriching companion these many years.

While Weil's work has been a fertile ground for political, philosophical, and theological studies, fewer literary scholars have made her the object of their study.[17] Katherine Brueck and Marie Cabaud Meaney focus on Weil's treatments of Greek tragedy; Brueck opposes Weil's supernatural, metaphysical readings, which argue for mystery and the enlightenment afforded by affliction, against structuralist and poststructuralist interpretations, which argue for the instability of the concepts "author," "reader," and "truth." Meaney studies Weil's essays on Greek tragedy as an "apologetics" of a kind, a bridge offering the believer access to a wider appreciation of the Catholic heritage by identifying Greek culture as an "intuition" of Christianity and offering the non-believer access to a rich cultural, literary locus from which to consider the treasures of Christianity. Both Joan Dargan and Thomas Stokes treat the "poetics" essential to Weil's writings, Dargan the figurative language and literary strategies that enact Weil's thought and structure a response on the part of the reader. She brings to our attention the constant "literary" choices Weil made in her writing and invites us to appreciate Weil the artificer by drawing parallels with other writers of literature. Stokes focuses on the "implied reader" Weil and Pascal fashion and address in their works. Both moved from more public *pièces d'occasion* (occasional pieces) to more private forms, notebooks and diaries. Who, he asks, is the intended audience of works written largely for private reflection? And who is the implied reader she constructs in her frequent use of the pronoun "nous"? Jane Doering and Ruthellen Johansen identify the complex intersection of thought and concerns of Weil and the fiction writer Flannery O'Connor and demonstrate how these are explored not only thematically by O'Connor but also are enacted by narrative and literary strategies. The two writers' shared concern with "the beauty of the world," for example, is signified in the fictional works of O'Connor by those cosmic elements that serve as background to temporal human beings' actions but of which humans are quite often unaware.

A number of scholars have explored the impact of Weil's thought on Iris Murdoch, for good reason: one major twentieth-century philosopher entered into a life-long dialogue with another. Most studies settle on those areas where Murdoch most freely acknowledged her debt: Weil's refraction of Plato, attention and decreation/unselfing as the center of the moral and epistemic act, and the intermediaries or *metaxu* serving to bridge the distance between God/the good and humans. Kate Larson addresses those important areas where divergences of terminology reveal divergences of thought: Murdoch's emphasis on "the good" and "spirituality" in contrast to Weil's focus on "God" and "Christianity."[18] Layla Raïd in turn distinguishes between the spiritual/moral disciplines of Weil's "prayer" and Murdoch's "contemplation."[19] Both Larson and Raïd reference Murdoch the novelist, who believed that literature "could illuminate the moral issues raised in systems of ethics."[20] Both, however, touch only lightly on the fiction.

Gabriele Griffin offers a monograph-length study of the two philosophers and more fully explores the impact of Weil's ideas on Murdoch's fiction, drawing on feminist theory to bring them into dialogue. At the core of what they share, according to Griffin, is their gender; they asserted themselves and excelled in the male-dominated realm of academe, successfully effecting an "intrusion into the male sphere."[21] They did so, according to Griffin, all the while refusing to acknowledge gender difference and the effect upon them of a patriarchal system and, importantly for Griffin, assimilating to the male gender.

Griffin argues that despite this unwillingness to identify as gendered female actors, the focus on "unselfing" and "attention" to others reveals a moral philosophy that follows a pattern laid out by Carol Gilligan—a female moral agent responsive to the needs of others rather than one that orders the world around his own needs and vision.

Griffin shows how this underlying moral philosophy informs Murdoch's novels—the problematic depiction of women as objects of male characters' concerns and desires but as having little agency of their own; the "good" characters as passive, often ineffectual watchers. A central focus is the "moral" effort Murdoch requires of her reader—given the ethically mixed or indeterminate characters and the number of novels that end without any satisfying "closure," the reader is left to do the work of drawing conclusions based on the material offered in the novels. The study offers for the most part a thematic and characterological study, with a hint of reader response.

My treatment is a novel one in that it brings both narrative theory and narrative psychology to bear on Weil's work. It also attempts to place Weil in a "thicker" historical and cultural context; I call up the historical moment, particularly between 1938 and 1943, to demonstrate how directly her thought engages with a broad circle of contemporaries: the widely read writers of her time, the popular press and the small-circulation political and union periodicals she wrote for and read, the study circles of *la France combattante*. This variegated picture of her contemporary culture throws her distinctive voice and insights into even sharper relief.

This study will focus on Weil's treatment of the official French historical narrative, the *sainte histoire* or sacred history propagated by the founders of the Third Republic. Robert Zaretsky notes with puzzlement the fact that Weil does not focus on history ("How odd, then, that Weil does not treat the study of history at length in any of her works").[22] His assertion evokes my own puzzlement. I will argue that from 1938 on France's history is a recurring concern in her works and elicits some of her most radical speculations. Any discussion of a country or a culture's roots, such as that found in Weil's final masterwork, *The Need for Roots*, requires tracing those roots backward in history. Eric Springsted's comment that "the notion of rootedness implies an emphasis on the historical, the distinctive, and the inevitably changing"[23] is a much more accurate assessment, to my mind.

If one group stubbornly defends the viability and robustness of France's "official" history directly after the Debacle (most often representatives of the left) another (most often the right) aims vicious kicks at its foundations. Both defenders and attackers acknowledge that history, however, as a powerful monolith, as the master narrative that defines the French comity. Weil takes a very critical stance toward this narrative: it is largely responsible for having "uprooted" the French, offering them a very thin and exhausted soil in which to take nourishment. But, in contrast to the other naysayers, Weil does not just throw pebbles at the monolith. Her analysis goes beyond binaries to dismantle it systematically and effectively. Since history is, in essence, narrative, a coherent story, narrative theory allows me to elucidate Weil's project by focusing on the strategies she uses. She arrives finally at a "liberation narrative," one that clears the ground for the possibility of another, different construct.

In the first chapter, we will look at the category of "master narratives." A term used by historians, sociologists, and psychologists, it encompasses those strategies and structures by which human beings organize "event" into "data," that is, transform it into knowledge. We will focus on the French master narrative written and championed by the Third Republic and study the ways it was propagated throughout the hexagon, inculcated largely through the educational system (particularly the teaching of history in primary and secondary schools).

The second chapter will focus on growing challenges to the master narrative in the 1930s—the pacifist movements and the 1939 celebration of the 150th anniversary of the Revolution. At the heart of the integral pacifist movement in France is a reworking of the Revolutionary heritage. Public festivals and celebrations are an important tool for propagating a regime's master narrative. The Radical government in power in 1939 hoped to use the commemoration to reaffirm their version of French history, whose origin is the Revolution; opponents of the Republic recast the Revolution as a tragic "wrong turn" and attempt to turn the celebration to their own purposes.

Chapter 3 will focus on those wartime responses to the master narrative that appeared after the defeat in 1940. In the view of those engaging in the debate, the fall of France offers a new piece of data that the master narrative must either absorb or shatter against.

This study relies on documents contemporary to the events discussed—textbooks, periodicals, journals, memoirs, and speeches—to follow the debates as they were occurring in the minds and imaginations of the French people. This "thick" context also enriches our understanding of Weil and her contributions. Much of what she published in her lifetime was written for specific publications with a particular readership in mind—she wrote, for example, the short essay on Antigone in *Entre nous*, a publication produced by the Rosière Foundary for its workers. Her discussion brings this tragedy into a contemporary context to allow it to resonate with her reader: Antigone resists the stiff-necked, vengeful king and pays with her life to grant her brother the burial that custom—and love—demands. Weil invites the reader to see the heroism involved in resistance to arbitrary and unjust power. Her articles on Occitanie in the *Les Cahiers du Sud* addressed a reader invested in a wider, more inclusive Mediterranean culture centered in the south, not the north of France. Her spiritual "autobiography" or testament, included in *L'Attente de Dieu* (Waiting for God), took the form of a letter to her spiritual mentor Father Perrin. It is tempting to see Weil's later writing as speaking over the messy present to eternity, as utopian, mapping all social and political concerns against spiritual imperatives. I attempt, by firmly situating her thought within a continuum of contemporary debates and documents, to demonstrate how richly conversant she was with that context and how directly she was speaking to the moment and her fellow French men and women even as she addresses eternity.

Throughout, certain themes and concerns will recur: the political divisions that tore the fabric of the French comity in that period; the hopelessly partisan press that fanned disunity and discord; the scapegoating of immigrants and newly naturalized citizens, blamed for some of the ills that were befalling the country; mass demonstrations and riots that sought to overturn the established government; and disgust with the political system and politicians. These are not unfamiliar elements to us as Americans living through the deep polarization of the 2020s. France in the 1930s and 1940s holds an interesting mirror up to present-day America.

I would like to express my deep gratitude to the two Weil societies, one in France and the other in the United States, that yearly bring together scholars from a range of different disciplines to engage in rich discussions of Weil and her work. In addition, the prefaces to all of the volumes of the *Oeuvres complètes*, under the guidance of Florence de Lussy, Robert Chenavier and the late André Devaux, surely among the most knowledgeable and insightful of all of Weil's readers, were most particularly important in helping me to situate Weil's concerns during the war as well as the historical and social context of those concerns. I relied in particular on the prefaces by Simone Fraisse (*Vers la guerre—Toward War*), Chenavier and Patrice Rolland (*The Need for Roots*), and Chenavier, Rolland, and Jean Riaud (*Questions politiques et religieuses—Political and Religious Questions*). Much of this study originated in exchanges of ideas that took place at those conferences and colloquies around the world. Most particular thanks go to Robert and Marie-Noëlle Chenavier, who together have been the mind, heart, and soul of the French Society for the study of Simone Weil's thought.

NOTES

1. Anne-Marie Thiesse, *Faire les Français: Quelle identité nationale?* (Paris: Stock, 2010), 49.
   This and all future translations from the French are those of the author.
2. Most major studies of Weil's work begin with an account of her life for just the reasons stated here: it intersects with a fraught historical moment, with which she engages fearlessly and directly: left-wing syndicalism, the pacifist movement, and the pivot to passionate engagement in the effort to liberate France and plan France's postwar future.
3. Simone Pétrement's two-volume study of Weil's life in French holds place of pride because of her friendship with Weil and her familiarity with the Weil family and the educational milieux that formed them both. (The edited one-volume edition in English is of necessity less complete.) Another biographical study written by those who knew her, Father Joseph-Marie Perrin and Gustave Thibon, treats a more restricted period and aspect of Weil's life. It focuses on her time in Marseille when she was immersing herself in spiritual inquiry through exchanges with the two authors, one a Dominican priest and the other active in Catholic circles. The authors

display a certain *parti pris*—had she lived to immerse herself more in Catholic teachings, they suggest, she well "might" have ended by accepting baptism. The book is also of interest as a study of Weil at a threshold moment of her life—deprived of her professional status by the Jewish statutes, preparing to leave for the United States, exploring spiritual life. Published first in 1952, it was written less than ten years after their acquaintance with Weil, so feels immediate. Jacques Cabaud published his biography of Weil in 1957, and because it was written not long after her death, he was able to speak to many who had known her. These three works have special resonance because of their proximity to Weil.

4. Simone Weil, "Allons-nous vers une revolution prolétarienne?" *Oeuvres complètes* II, Vol. 1 (Paris: Gallimard, 1988), 272.

All future citations from the *Oeuvres complètes* will be abbreviated *OC*.

It is instructive to consider the work of Michael Sandel, who criticizes the premises and workings of the meritocracy (*The Tyranny of Merit*)—what worth and value are granted to, and are felt by, those who are not able to scramble to the top of the meritocratic social pyramid?

5. "machine bureaucratique et militaire."
Weil, "Allons-nous," 264.
6. Weil, "Allons-nous," 265.
7. "Quand ils ont fait le désert, ils appellent cela la paix."
Simone Weil, "Quelques réflexions sur les origines de *l'hitlérisme*," *OC* II, Vol. 3 (Paris: Gallimard, 1989), 203.
8. Simone Weil, "Autobiographie spirituelle," in *Attente de Dieu*, ed. J.-M. Perrin (Paris: Fayard, 1967), 34.
9. Weil, "Autobiographie," 37.
10. "Parce que le malheur et la vérité ont besoin pour être entendus de la même attention, l'esprit de justice et l'esprit de vérité ne font qu'un."
Simone Weil, "La Personne et le sacré," *OC* V, Vol. 1 (Paris: Gallimard, 2019), 231.
11. Simone Weil, "L'Amour de Dieu et le malheur," *OC* IV, Vol. 1 (Paris: Gallimard, 2008), 369.
12. "La distance infinie qui sépare Dieu et la créature se rassemble toute entière en un point pour percer une âme en son centre."
Weil, "L'Amour de Dieu," 359.
13. "tuent les âmes."
Weil, "L'Amour de Dieu," 349.
14. Iris Murdoch, *The Nice and Good* (New York: Penguin, 1968), 56.
15. "tués, tortures, chassés de leur pays, réduits à la misère et à l'esclavage, confinés dans des camps ou cachots."
Weil, "L'Amour de Dieu," 348.
16. Robert Chenavier, "Personal Identity and National Identity: An Analogy," *Philosophical Investigations* 43, no. 1–2 (January 1, 2020): 158. doi:10.1111/phin.12266.
17. Katherine Brueck, *The Redemption of Tragedy: The Literary Vision of Simone Weil* (Albany, NY: SUNY Press, 1995); Thomas Stokes, *Audience, Intention, and*

Rhetoric in Pascal and Simone Weil (New York; Washington, DC; Baltimore: Peter Lang, 1996); Joan Dargan, *Simone Weil: Thinking Poetically* (Albany, NY: SUNY Press, 1998); Marie Cabaud Meaney, *Simone Weil's Apologetic Use of Literature* (Oxford: Oxford University Press, 2007); E. Jane Doering and Ruthann Knechel Johansen, *When Fiction and Philosophy Meet: A Conversation with Flannery O'Connor and Simone Weil* (Macon, GA: Mercer University Press, 2019).

18. Kate Larson, "'The Most Intimate Bond': Metaxological Thinking in Simone Weil and Iris Murdoch," in *Iris Murdoch Connected: Critical Essays on Her Fiction and Philosophy* (University of Tennessee Press, 2014).

19. Layla Raïd, "Iris Murdoch et Simone Weil: l'attention," in *Mélanges en l'honneur de René Daval* (EPURE. Éditions et Presses Universitaires de Reims, 2019).

20. Sissela Bok, "Simone Weil and Iris Murdoch: The Possibility of a Dialogue," *Gender Issues* 22, no. 4 (2005): 77. doi: 10.1007/s12147-005-0006-2.

21. Gabriele Griffin, *The Influence of the Writings of Simone Weil on the Fiction of Iris Murdoch* (Lewiston, NY: Edwin Mellen Press, 1993), 71.

22. Robert Zaretsky, *The Subversive Simone Weil: A Life in Five Ideas* (Chicago: University of Chicago Press, 2021), 125.

23. Eric Springsted, *Simone Weil for the Twenty-First Century* (South Bend, IN: University of Notre Dame Press, 2021), 165, Epub.

Chapter 1

Historical Narrative and the Founding of the French Third Republic

The French Third Republic existed from 1871 through 1940. Military defeat at the hands of the Germans precipitated its birth and its death: in 1871 the Second Empire of Napoleon III crumbled after France's defeat in the Franco-Prussian War, and the Third Republic was declared in its wake; in July of 1940 the Third Republic was voted out of existence by its elected representatives after France's capitulation to Nazi Germany and full powers were put into the hands of Marshall Philippe Pétain as head of the French State.

The Third Republic was by far the longest of France's experiments with constitutional democracy to that date. The First Republic, established after the abolishment of the monarchy in 1792, ended in 1804 with Napoleon I's declaration of the French Empire, although it had already passed through periods that little resembled a democracy (i.e., the dictatorship of the Committee of Public Safety during the Terror of 1793 to 1794; the one-man autocracy of Napoleon's consulship from 1799 to 1804); the Second Republic, declared after the Revolution of 1848, was abolished after Louis Napoleon's coup in 1851, and the Second Empire was approved by plebiscite the following year.

Such a track record of short-lived experiments with representative democracy gave the founders of the Third Republic pause. As the historian Mona Ozouf expressed it, "To proclaim a Republic in France, *that* [emphasis in original] the French know how to do, they do it from time to time. On the other hand, for a century they showed themselves incapable of making one last."[1]

The founders of the Third Republic were fully aware of this lamentable track record and of the long-standing antagonisms that would continue to challenge its existence: monarchists (including legitimists, Orleanists, and Bonapartists[2]), the Catholic Church and radical socialists formed a solid wall of opposition at its creation, and many of these same groups would work against it through its entire existence. The founders were intent on precluding yet another violent overthrow of a French Republic by its opponents. It was essential that this third iteration win the allegiance and even love of the French people. Republican policies, institutions, and lore had to become so inextricably intertwined in the fabric of the nation that it would be impossible to imagine France without them.

The founders undertook a concerted effort to forge a nation out of disparate regions and distinctive populations, to create a comity out of a people for whom the term "republic" held little magic and attracted less fealty. They rendered the will-o'-the-wisp entity "the Republic" increasingly corporeal and solid through a panoply of different strategies. Jean-Pierre Azéma and Michel Winock focus a large section of their history of the Third Republic on the "ideological cement" its leaders mixed and hoped to see solidify. At its inception, the Republic was supported by a large party of "the satisfied"—the peasantry, the bourgeoisie, the small business owners, and civil servants—whose interests were well served by the "bourgeois republic" and whose numbers outweighed those in opposition, the remnants of the *Ancien Régime* and the far left.[3] But "satisfaction" could not alone create the comity they envisioned. If the French Revolution had left France a land of "irreconcilable families" once the cohesive element of Church had disappeared,[4] one of the founders' first tasks was to replace that lost "spiritual cement" with another, just as effective in binding together a disparate population. The Republic was tasked with gathering the French into a belief community similar to an organized religion, making use of many of the same strategies to unify the believers. "It is through its intellectual seduction, the symbols it incarnates, the ideals it proclaims, the enemies it denounces, in the affection and faithfulness toward itself that it aroused that the Third Republic found a solid principle of continuity."[5]

At the center of these strategies was a concerted campaign to evoke a past, a shared history through which a national identity could be cast. The founders already knew what Simone Weil confirmed in 1943: "To love France, one must feel it has a past."[6] This study will focus on the narrative of the past fashioned by the French Republic, a past through which the French were invited to love their country. It will explore the "sacred history" of the Republic that held sway in France from, approximately, the late 1800s on, focusing particularly on its contested status in the late 1930s through the early 1940s.

The founders expressed enormous confidence in this sacred history's role in ensuring the success of the newly formed Republic. It was tasked with presenting the French a coherent narrative of their national past, within which individual identities as citizens as well as the shared identity of the comity would form. And to a large degree it met that challenge. How was Republican sacred history able to effect this sea change? How can a history, crafted in narrative form, structure the way people make sense of historical events and of their place within those events, so that "my history" can only be understood within the "larger history . . . through which one's life assumes its distinctive form"?[7] How can it lead a fractious population to understand themselves as members of a comity? How can it instill love and loyalty toward the nation? Narrative theory and narrative psychology help to illuminate the elements of the particularly pervasive narrative of French history forged by the founders of the Third Republic.

We will take "narrative" to encompass written texts and, as importantly for the purposes of this study, unwritten narratives shared by a society, "master narratives" that serve as preexisting scaffolds within which one organizes "experiences" or "events." Comprising a coherent whole, with beginnings, intermediary material connected through cause and effect, and an end that is consonant with what has preceded, they exist as social and cultural blueprints and furnish the "received" patterns onto which members of a society map their experience of the world.

The following exposition will treat the theorists and elements of narrative theory most helpful for this study: the literary strategies that create something we recognize as a narrative, the way narratives function to order meaning and enable understanding of experience, the danger of a "totalizing" master narrative that not only explicates but also constrains, and the possibility of responding to such totalizing master narratives with counternarratives.

The strategies and function of narrative have attracted the interest of scholars from a range of different fields. Predictably, literary theory established the foundations for the academic study of narrative, and later theorists gesture back, at the very least, to that base.

Formalists (e.g., Vladimir Propp in *The Morphology of the Folk Tale*) remind us of how we recognize a text as a narrative at all, the elements that signal we are in the presence of a "tale"—the "initial situation" that spurs the tale into being (i.e., in the case of the folk tale perhaps a couple's childlessness or an interdiction), the "functions" or "spheres of action" of different character types (the hero, the donor, and the villain), their "motivations" or "reasons and aims," the narrative "units" and their combination through "conjunctive" moments or integuments, and the way closure is achieved.

At the center of formalist theory is the distinction between plot and story, where the *story* consists of the bare, chronicle-like "events" which the *plot* fashions into an artifact. As Viktor Schklovsky reminds his reader in *The Theory of Prose*, the *story* holds little interest for the theorist, whose attention is drawn by the more ingenious, revelatory plot. He goes so far as to claim, "As a matter of fact, though, the story line is nothing more than material for plot formation."[8] Schklovsky's critical attention is captured by those works that eschew "story" almost entirely, or at least problematize it—*Tristram*

Shandy and *Don Quixote*, which with their numerous interpolations and digressions manage to almost overwrite the story; the detective novel which most often elides the primary scene, the commission of the crime, reconstructing it only later. Rather than slavishly following the "story line," the plot "distorts" it "by the very fact that it selects it, and on the basis of rather arbitrary criteria."[9]

Propp and Schklovsky focus on the folk tale and the novel, but their observations on the workings of these literary narratives illuminate our study of historical narratives in the following areas: the distinction between plot and story; the focus on what constitutes an "event" and the importance of the initial, propulsive event; the "natural" laws that govern cause and effect in the sequence of events; the roles distributed to "heroes," "villains," and "donor" characters; and, as the culmination of these intertwined sequences, the determination of what constitutes a satisfactory "ending." These theorists demand that we remain mindful of how much art there is involved in taking the "story" and creating a "plot" out of it.

The archetypal criticism of Northrop Frye offers a means to attach these strategies, structures, and character types to a societal context. Frye explores the *kinds* of stories these strategies and structures construct and argues that all literary stories fall into one of the following modes—Comedy, Tragedy, Irony, or Romance. Each reflects different societal groupings that tend to predominate in different ages, and each forefronts different heroes and different antagonists who act within those groupings. Depending upon that specific moment, the society will see itself mirrored in a specific kind of story, which entails the heroes, antagonists, and endings appropriate to that mode.

The society of Tragedy is that "controlled by habit, ritual bondage, arbitrary law and older characters,"[10] where the hero is defeated and kept outside of a societal construct that proves too brittle to accommodate them. And if, on the contrary, the hero, despite their original outsider status, proves able to transform and "redeem" a society, transform it into one "controlled by youth and pragmatic freedom" by their very entry to it, we are in the realm of Comedy.[11]

The historian Hayden White brings a formalist/structuralist approach, as well as the archetypal criticism of Northrop Frye, to bear on the historical narratives of the nineteenth century. His approach shares the formalist emphasis on the existence of a set of "primitive elements" available to the storyteller from which they can "select" and which they can "arrange." In the case of an historian, these elements are data from "the unprocessed historical record."

> Indeed, it is only by troping [i.e., employment of literary devices], rather than by logical deduction, that any given set of the kinds of past event we would wish to call historical can be (first) *represented* [emphases in original] as having

the order of a chronicle; (second) *transformed* by emplotment into a story with identifiable beginning, middle, and end phases; and (third) *constituted* [emphases in original] as a subject of whatever formal arguments may be adduced to establish their meaning.[12]

The "mode" of the narrative, whether Comedy, Tragedy, Romance, or Irony, is determinative both for the selection and the arrangement of this data.

> A certain plot type (tragedy) can simultaneously determine the kinds of events to be featured in any story that can be told about them and provide a pattern for the assignment of the roles that can possibly be played by the agents and agencies inhabiting the scene thus constituted.[13]

By the logic of the mode chosen, the "primitive elements" at hand are selected out; within its framework, the events are "emplotted." Thanks to these processes of selection and emplotment, the reader is "provided with a story"[14] which is revealed to be "a story of a particular kind."[15]

White asserts that the mode of historical writing that obtained in nineteenth-century Europe was Comedy. He further argues that this mode can best be understood as a legacy of the greater master narrative provided by the Enlightenment, "'optimism' and the doctrine of progress which usually accompanied it."[16]

He cites Kant's philosophy of history and discusses the philosopher's justification of the choice of the Comic mode in the following terms:

> Kant's reasons for opting for this Comic notion of the meaning of the whole process were ultimately ethical ones. The spectacle of history had to be conceived as a Comic drama or else men would fail to take up those Tragic projects which alone can transform chaos into a meaningful field of human endeavor.[17]

Interestingly, White emphasizes the fact that the choice of the Comic mode is not perhaps the most "accurate" way of seeing "human endeavor" but is hortatory: only by imagining a better, transformed world will human beings find the heart to brave the tragic troughs of event and carry on with the work of human development.

> The reconciliations that occur at the end of Comedy are reconciliations of men with men, of men with their world and their societies; the condition of society is represented as being purer, saner, and healthier as a result of the conflict among seemingly inalterably opposed elements of in the world.[18]

Nineteenth-century historical narratives, White argues, situate the reader firmly within the transformed world of Frye's Comedy; they reflect the

Enlightenment master narrative from which they derive, the frameworks of optimism and progress.

The archetypal approach of Frye and White remains at the level of "epochs" and "generations"; they offer models for understanding the macrostructures that order a society's view of itself. How to span the distance between the epochal and the more narrowly historical, a specific culture in a specific time frame? The concept of "collective memory" as well as the field of narrative psychology will allow us to study how macrostructures penetrate to the level of smaller groupings, even individuals; they offer a way of bridging the distance between "master narratives" and "life scripts." How this bridging was scaffolded during the Third Republic will be the focus of this study.

The primary tenet of narrative psychology is that all human knowledge is in fact narrative. Michael White argues the following:

> that culture is socially and historically constructed, that narrative is a primary, in humans perhaps *the* [emphasis in original] primary mode of knowing, that we assemble the selves we live in out of materials lying about in the society around us and develop a theory of mind to comprehend the selves of others, that we do not act directly on the world but on beliefs we hold about the world, that from birth on we are all active, impassioned meaning makers in search of plausible stories, and that mind cannot in any sense be regarded as natural or naked, with culture thought of as an add-on.[19]

The proponents of narrative psychology give no quarter to post-modern skepticism toward explanatory narratives. Narrative sense-making, they argue, proceeds on two levels simultaneously: there are the life scripts that individuals create out of the materials of their individual experience, and these life scripts are shaped within the master narratives that prevail at a specific moment. If the life scripts provide the recognizable events, the "primary materials," they find meaning and coherence only in reference to the prevailing master narrative. As Kate McLean and her collaborators specify, any master narrative must, to function as such, possess certain characteristics: they must be ubiquitous, that is, "known by the majority"; they must prove useful in offering "valued frameworks for defining the self"; they must be "invisible," that is, internalized to such a degree that the possessors are "unaware that they are conforming to cultural expectations"; and be rigid, "difficult to change."[20]

Narrative psychology gestures to and assumes the more formalist, structuralist treatments of narrative in its emphasis upon temporal unfolding, different set story "memes," and the narrative logic that connects them. "Narratives provide a sequential organisation that specifies the unfolding of an event along temporal lines, but even more so, narratives provide an explanatory and evaluative framework for understanding how and why events unfold as they do."[21]

The work of the philosopher Maurice Halbwachs offers another connected concept for understanding how the behemoth master narrative, the archetypal "mode," intersects with the individual as well as the smaller, chronologically specific groups to which those individuals belong. Halbwachs uses the term "collective memory" to denote what the members of a group share: they might be far separated in geography, class, or specific individual experiences, but they all swim in "a current of social thought . . . as invisible as the atmosphere we breath."[22] Halbwachs, who was a young child in France during the early years of the Third Republic and so didn't remember the events of that period as a participant or even a knowledgeable spectator, argues that he shares a "collective memory" of the events by the very fact of being part of the larger French comity:

> These events have deeply influenced national thought, not only because they have altered institutions but also because their traditions endure, very much alive, in region, province, political party, occupation, class, even certain families or persons who experience them firsthand. For me they are conceptions, symbols . . . I can imagine them, but I cannot remember them. I belong to a group with a part of my personality, so that everything that has occurred within it as long as I belonged—even everything that interested and transformed it before I entered—is in some sense familiar to me.[23]

Mark Freeman's work resonates with aspects of Halbwachs's. Freeman uses the term "narrative unconscious" to suggest the way these larger narratives imbue and inform the individual psyche. As opposed to the Freudian "unconscious," the narrative unconscious is not repressed, "banished to the nether reaches of the psyche."[24] It is instead a point of intersection, where "my history" meets "larger history."[25]

As members of a larger community, this unconscious is an essential element of our "very existence as historical beings."[26] Although not firsthand participants in all that has preceded a group's history, all members possess a "second-order autobiographical memory" by the very fact of existing in that group. These "outside sources" become part of our memory banks; we have, as it were, absorbed them through our very pores.

> With first-order autobiographical memory, there is at least an "anchor," so to speak, of actuality, however schematically and conventionally this actuality may be viewed. With second order autobiographical memory . . . the anchor is gone; and in its place is a kind of montage, a poetically figured heterogeneous image, rounded off the edges.[27]

It is this process that the following study will explore: how the master narrative of progress, written in the mode of Comedy, was created and instilled in the French by the founders of the Third Republic and their successors; how it created in the French a sense of themselves as a group, on both more conscious levels (collective memory, second-order autobiographical memory) and unconscious levels (narrative unconscious). We will follow both the creation (after 1871) and the devolving of that master narrative (between 1938 and 1943). Like all life scripts, it served to order and illuminate and, eventually, could be seen to limit and proscribe. As Julie Beck asked in an *Atlantic* article in which she reviewed the literature on narrative psychology,

> So what to do, then, with all the things that don't fit tidily? There is evidence that finding some "unity" in your narrative identity is better, psychologically, than not finding it. And it probably is easier to just drop those things as you pull patterns from the chaos, though it may take some readjusting.[28]

Not all agree that "dropping" those elements that can't easily fit into a unified narrative is the best alternative, as we shall see.

In his classic treatment *Peasants into Frenchmen*, Eugen Weber focuses on those policies and institutions that forged a "territorial unit" and "cultural jigsaw" into a "nation" and "Republic" after 1871.[29] Much work toward this unification had been initiated earlier in terms of expanding educational opportunities for young children, and in so doing forcing them to abandon their patois and learn French, and improving transportation (passable roads and railways) between areas that before had remained inaccessible to each other. The Third Republic speeded these developments along, in large part in order to establish the new Republic as essential, ubiquitous, and worthy of loyalty and adhesion. Central to this program was encouraging a "national" over a local or regional identity, forging and transmitting those "common ideas" that allow a comity to form.

And the whole hinged on schooling. The founders realized the challenge it would entail to "teach the peasantry that Alsace and Lorraine mattered to them"[30] or to convince the French that, in President Léon Gambetta's words, "There is a moral entity to which [a man] must give all, sacrifice all, his life, his future, and that this entity . . . is France."[31]

The founders of the Third Republic waged a concerted campaign to improve the reach and efficacy of education and to wrest it from the clutches of religious authorities: between 1881 and 1886, many public elementary schools were built to ensure children even in small communes had access; all fees were abolished, bringing elementary education within the reach of all economic classes; training programs for elementary school teachers were instituted; and a strict secularism was observed.[32]

Jules Ferry, twice president of the new Republic and its first minister of Public Instruction, had seen from a front-row seat the sorry fate of the short-lived Second Republic, a trauma that haunted him for the rest of his life. As late as 1887 he still recounted the day of Louis Napoleon's 1851 coup d'état as a fresh wound.

> My friends, men of my age have seen terrible things. I saw, when I was very young, just out of school, I saw December 2nd! I saw soldiers, disoriented, maybe bribed, shoot republicans and even innocent bystanders on the boulevards. I saw working class men, blind or unaware, snicker as the National Assembly passed by on their way to Maza [a prison in Paris].[33]

He was intent that the Third Republic not end in similar ignominy and was convinced education held a central place in its safeguarding. He blamed the 1848 vote for Louis Napoleon and his brand of "Caesarism" not on "inequality in conditions" but "inequality in education."[34]

Ferry's espousal of positivism informed his program; education was instrumental in instilling "positive knowledge and values," in "indoctrinating" all members of society to bring it from a "religious" to a "positivist" stage of development. A new type of French citizen could be scientifically "constructed" with the concerted efforts of all society's institutions, including schools and the family.[35]

The project to establish Republican schools overseen by Republican authorities that taught Republican history was hard-fought and its enactment into law a slow slog in the 1880s.[36]

As minister of Public Instruction, Ferry worked to ensure that the development of young minds be firmly in the hands of a secular rather than religious authority, that teachers were qualified and vetted by a state jealous of its educational prerogatives, not beholden to any religious authority as had been the case through "letters of obedience" (*lettres d'obédience*) granted to instructors in religious institutions. Alfred Rambaud, himself later the Minister of Public Instruction and an intimate of Ferry, in his biography of his friend offers examples of Jesuit school texts pre-1875 that praise or at least give a pass to the Inquisition, the Saint Bartholomew's Day massacres of protestants in 1572, and the revocation of the Edict of Nantes in 1685, an edict which assured freedom of worship and civil liberties to French protestants.[37] The educational policy of the new Republic was intent on eliminating such sectarian instruction. Given the arc of French history presented by the Republican narrative, which enshrined the displacement of the monarchy and nobility and the sidelining of the overweening influence of the Catholic Church, it is predictable that these groups comprising the Counter-Revolution offered the stiffest resistance to the new educational policies and priorities. In the words of Pascal Dupuy, they stood sullenly against what the Revolution represented: "the principal of national or popular sovereignty"; "civil equality," which in its emphasis on individualism threatened "the natural family"; "Promethean rationalism"; and the rejection of sacredness in preference for "progress" and "happiness."[38]

Ferry understood that compulsory education would be central to ensuring the durability of the new Republic that it would serve to "recast the national soul," to instill "a collective fervor," and to animate a "community life."[39] The teaching of history, and its corollary geography, took the preeminent role in making the Republic real to students and creating loyalty toward it. These two subjects were seen as effective "instruments of indoctrination and patriotic conditioning," as "an instrument of unity."[40]

The teachers of the Third Republic were seen as its best representatives, the missionaries who brought the "good news" of the Republic out to the unenlightened or unbelievers, the avant-garde prepared to proselytize among those populations who did not even consider themselves properly "French" but instead spoke their patois and considered their village or *pays* the ambit of their ambitions, who saw the Republic as far-removed from their everyday concerns. It is not hard to understand why the teaching corps held to the Republic with such devotion; once they became civil servants answerable only to the central government, they were liberated from the surveillance of the town curé, mayor, and municipal council, who could no longer fire them, and their salaries were increased. Antoine Prost and Jacques and Mona Ozouf recount anecdotes shared by the first generation of Republican teachers about the indignities to which they were too often exposed at the hands of local notables.[41] Azéma and Winock observe that the changed status of teachers conferred on them a new "social dignity."[42]

These teachers were responsible for turning "peasants into Frenchmen" in their classrooms, for instilling in their students a sense of French identity and patriotism, for encouraging a love for the fatherland, and all largely through the teaching of French history. The Ozoufs observe that "The teaching of the history of France was supposed therefore to be the site for the staging of national unity."[43] Weber describes the shift from Empire to Republic in teaching in the following terms:

> [Teachers taught or were expected to teach] not just for the love of art or science . . . but for the love of France—a France whose creed had to be inculcated in all unbelievers. A Catholic God, particularist and only identified with the Fatherland by revisionists after the turn of the century, was replaced by a secular God: the Fatherland and its living symbols, the army and the flag. Catechism was replaced by civics lessons. Biblical history, proscribed in secular schools, was replaced by the sainted history of France. French became more than a

possession of the educated: it became a patrimony in which all could share with significant results for national cohesion, as in 1914 war would show.[44]

It was at first difficult for the teachers to serve as proselytizers for the Republic, the *patrie*, given that many of them had not studied French history themselves and had to race to keep a step ahead of their students' knowledge.[45] The socialist leader Jean Jaurès pointed out the need to first educate the educator: "The teacher must be imbued by what he teaches. He should not repeat in the afternoon what he learned that morning."[46]

This gap explains the central role played by the historian Ernest Lavisse, a noted and prolific professor at both the *École Normale Supérieure* and later the Sorbonne, whose handbooks of French history, revised and reprinted from 1881 well into the twentieth century, defined the teaching of French history during the Third Republic.

Lavisse's influence reached into virtually every primary, secondary, and college classroom in France for over 30 years thanks to his textbooks written for these various levels of instruction. Lavisse would have heartily agreed with Weil about the importance of young French students coming to love their country through its history: "For it is my deep conviction that the only way to save France is to give to the young specific reasons to love their country and their duties toward it. . . . And French democracy will finally be a reality!"[47] It lays in the hands of Republican teachers to inculcate this love and sense of responsibility in their students. "But one hundred years have not proven enough to have liberty penetrate spirits, which would be the culmination of the French Revolution. You can do that through giving particular attention to moral and physical instruction."[48]

Textbooks were created to meet the new learning standards drawn up by the Ministry of Public Instruction. The most widely adopted history text, the most intertwined with the Republican project, was Lavisse's book geared to elementary students. It offers a clear picture of the civic values being inculcated and the master narrative of French history being laid out. These tenets, present in this textbook for the youngest students, were reinforced in all of Lavisse's subsequent textbooks geared to other ages. The Republican version of French history identified a number of large themes in its narrative of progress, which Lavisse identifies in a series of articles on teaching. He highlights the creation of a unified nation out of scattered regions, largely through the monarchy's annexation and centralization of power ("We will then show the unification of France by the continuous progress of royal authority"[49]); the centralization of power away from a fractious nobility into the hands of the monarch;[50] the importance of improvements and technological progress in terms of ports, roads, commerce, railways, all of which brought far-flung areas in closer connection;[51] the French Revolution, despite its excesses (regicide, the September massacres), as opening the way to a modern France of rights and limits to government power ([T]he French Revolution made an heroic effort to substitute the reign of justice and reason for the ancient monarchy . . . which instituted a new era in the world, and which recast, if you will, almost all of Europe[52]); and France's policy of colonization as a "civilizing" mission ("France wants little Arabs to be as well educated as little French children. This proves that our France is good and generous to those peoples it has subjugated"[53]).

This master narrative, this official "sacred history," was strikingly successful at propagating what Azéma and Winock term the new Republic's "ideological cement." If the Third Republic's keywords were "progress" and "liberty," one of its principal tasks was to show these as defining threads in French history. Republican historiography enshrines the Revolution's centrality as both a watershed and boundary dividing *ancien* from modern France, casting that event as a heroic line of development from the taking of the Bastille to the rising of an entire people against "the coalition of the despots";[54] it casts Republicanism and the Third Republic in particular as representing the culmination of a certain development and logic of French (and indeed world) history; it identifies progress with increased centralization and the widening authority of the state; it sets itself up as an example to prove that social change and equality can be achieved through peaceful and even governmental means and deliberative bodies rather than revolution and violence. Reason and science constitute the motors behind this transformation. A gamut of Republican institutions and national spectacles and holidays supported this sacred history, including the most significant of Third Republic commemorative holidays, Bastille Day.

This history effectively galvanized a people and forged a nation. Narrative theory and narrative psychology can help us understand its particular power. The French Revolution, a world historical event of unparalleled import, serves to impel the narrative. Although Lavisse reaches back to ancient Gaul and forward to the twentieth century, the Revolution serves as the pivot of his history. As the Ozoufs assert,

> Defined as the birth certificate of the true France, the Revolution becomes the privileged observation point from which one will judge . . . the events and the characters of history; after 1789, one approves what carries forward the Revolution; but before 1789, one attempts to discover what heralds it.[55]

The annexation of territories, the centralization of power, and the monarch's increased authority over a fractious nobility, those moments when authority and rights are wrested away from the nobility and the monarch and ceded to the people, all "herald" the Revolution. And the Third Republic represents its natural apotheosis.

The actors, both heroes and villains, are likewise selected to represent "proto-Republican" virtues and anti-Republican failings. Lavisse holds up for admiration those many military figures who protected France from invaders—Vercingetorix and Joan of Arc, naturally, but also common men of uncommon valor. In addition, he cites figures such as Saint Louis, who meted out justice equitably, without regard to the station of the plaintiffs or defendants. The villains are those invaders who threaten the integrity of France, but more insidiously the great lords whose incessant squabbles devastated France and caught its people in the crush. The monarch's efforts to rein in their prerogatives are seen as significant progress. Too often, though, a monarch can in his excesses harm France—Louis XIV in his profligate spending and wars, Napoleon in his overweening and ultimately disastrous military ambitions. An autocrat, despite the good he might have accomplished during his reign, is a danger to France. The populace's desire for the right to govern themselves leads inexorably, of course, to the French Revolution. And the French Revolution finds its apotheosis in the establishment of the Third Republic, which constitutes the satisfying conclusion to the narrative.

And what kind of identity are the French invited to derive from this history? They are invited to see themselves and their life scripts within this narrative of progress and consider themselves, as French citizens, to be not only happy heirs of a process but actors in motoring it. They are at the forefront of progress, politically, of course, but also scientifically and technologically (a natural corollary to political progress), as the Universal Exposition of 1889, coinciding with the centenary of the French Revolution, was intended to prove handily. World history was impelled forward by the Revolution when the French people rose up to defeat the "coalition of despots." The citizen is invited to take their place within this heroic lineage. Because of their agency, they achieved the best of all possible governments—a Republic—and *their* Republic, as many assure them, is the *best* of all possible republics. Jean Jaurès voices this view powerfully in his 1893 article "France and Socialism" ("La France et le socialisme"):

> If we, French socialists, if we remained indifferent to the honor, the security, the prosperity of France, it would not be a crime merely against the fatherland that we would be committing, but we would be committing a crime against humanity, because France, a free, great and strong France, is necessary to humanity. It's in France that democracy has reached its most logical form, the Republic; and, if France fell, the forces of reaction would rise in the world. It's in France,

in the country of the Revolution, that the return of tyrannies, feudal or clerical, is the most difficult.[56]

But the people at the avant-garde of history must remain hypervigilant against retrograde forces. Other enduring villains of this French narrative are the Germans, portrayed in Lavisse as natural, historical antagonists ("The Germans are a very arrogant people. They are always looking for an opportunity to do us harm"[57]), and the 1871 defeat and the loss of Alsace and Lorraine are but the last incidents in a long enmity, in his account. Lavisse insists upon the fact that patriotism is synonymous with military readiness, and he intersperses throughout his textbooks stories about individuals, both humble and great, who distinguish themselves by their military bravery in the face of an invading enemy. The last lines of this primary school textbook read as an exhortation as well as something close to a warning to Germany: "General officers, infantry, cavalry, all know their profession. If France is attacked, all will do their duty. *France is well defended* [emphasis in original]."[58]

This *revanchisme* sounds as an even louder drumbeat in the textbook of Charles Bigot, *Le Petit Français*, published in 1884 and widely adopted as a manual to instill patriotism. Here, the writer pounds into his young readers' minds the humiliation inflicted upon France in 1870—he exhorts them to remember the dates of lost battles: Sedan, Metz, Champigny;[59] he enumerates the numbers of dead and injured and outlines the punishing terms of the armistice—the onerous reparations and, the most devastating, "the black marks" on the map that used to be Alsace and Lorraine.[60] In a particularly manipulative maneuver, he warns his young (male) readers that women look approvingly on brave men in uniform.

> There is not one mother who would rather see her son dead than dishonored. A young man who has shied away from military service, a soldier who has stepped back from his duty, can be as handsome and rich as possible: they are without honor in the eyes of women and young girls. If women love the military uniform, it's because for them it's synonymous with courage.[61]

As Henry Rousso reminds us, "History is not the mortar out of which an artificial unity can be created—unless the mortar is mixed with that express purpose in mind."[62] And the men overseeing the crafting of the historical narrative had that purpose clearly in mind. Ferry and his fellow Minister of Public Instruction Paul Bert, both close readers of August Comte and his positivist philosophy, believed it was experimentally and scientifically possible to educate students into Republicanism through the teaching of history. As Prost writes,

> Above all, the problem of constituting the nation was placed on history. In the mind of a Lavisse, or of statesmen such as H. Ferry or P. Bert, it was a deliberate

choice, an attempt to found a cult of the fatherland within which partisans and adversaries of the Revolution were reconciled.[63]

As Dominique Maingueneau has demonstrated, the teaching of sacred history and the duties of citizenship were not relayed only through history texts and classes but reinforced in French language courses as well, in what we now call "the language arts." The most widely utilized French grammar textbook from 1889 through the end of World War I was Hanriot and Huleux's *Cours régulier de langue française (cours intermédiare) (Regular course of French language (intermediate level))*. Maingueneau examines the exercises and examples chosen to convey rhetoric and grammar and concludes that they supported the Republican "ideology" taught in history lessons. Many of the incidents and figures drawn upon were historical in nature and the exercises assumed a grasp of historical issues beyond mere rote familiarity.

Even an anodyne lesson on the use of adjectives ending in *-er* serves as a springboard for reaffirming the character of the French citizen. The adjectives *guerrier* (warlike) and *léger* (light) offer the opportunity to discuss the French as a "warlike nation and people" (*un peuple guerrier/une nation guerrière*) and to contest the accusation often leveled against them as being "light." The people are, instead, "proud of their freedom" (*fier de sa liberté*).[64]

A contemporary of Ernest Lavisse, Ernest Renan, was contemplating the nation and the Republic from a different but complementary vantage point. If Lavisse was constructing a history commensurate to the new Republic, Renan was considering how this construction in fact formed citizens. What function does historical "data" play in creating a sense of nation and a sense of a unified "people"? How does one historical narrative assert itself, and how does it assure a people's allegiance to it? Renan, an *agrégé* in philosophy who distinguished himself in the fields of philology and sociology as well, published a collection of articles in 1872 under the title *La Réforme intellectuelle et morale (Intellectual and Moral Reform)*. In this collection he considers the disaster that the Franco-Prussian War represented for France, how maimed she felt after the loss of Alsace and Lorraine, and how she might proceed thereafter. He includes in the collection an exchange with his own mentor David Friedrich Strauss, an apologist for the annexation of Alsace by Germany after the war. In his response, Renan refuses the claim that the ethnic origin or language spoken by a population should determine its nationality.[65] A nation and national identity, Renan retorts, are comprised of much more than mere language and ethnicity. This assertion serves as a jumping-off point for *Qu'est-ce qu'une nation? (What Is a Nation?)*, a speech given in 1882 in which he proposes other bases upon which France could be reconstituted after the defeat of 1871 and the amputation of Alsace and Lorraine.

Renan begins that speech by categorically refusing certain notions of what constitutes "a nation"—it is not coextensive with a race, with a language, with a shared religion, with any material, economic interest (i.e., the German *Zollverein* or Customs Union). Renan makes the claim that "nothing material suffices. A nation is a spiritual principle, resulting from profound complications of history, a spiritual family, not a group determined by the configuration of the soil."[66]

Renan, like Ferry, was a close reader of Comte He brought down on his head the Church's opprobrium for applying the sciences to the understanding of the figure of Jesus Christ in his *Vie de Jésus* (*Life of Jesus*). His claim, then, that "nothing material," not even geography or "the configuration of the soil" suffices to constitute a nation, that its essence is "spiritual," might surprise, and he feels compelled to explain what he understands by that adjective:

> In fact, two things, which really come down to one, constitute this soul, this spiritual principle. One is in the past, the other in the present. One is the possession in common of a rich legacy of memories; the other is a present consent, the desire to live together, the will to continue to affirm the heritage received intact.[67]

What constitutes this past, this "rich legacy of memories" necessary to the creation of a nation? "An historic past, great men, glory (and by that I mean true glory), that is the social capital upon which a national idea rests."[68] The story woven out of these "great figures" and "glories" is, essentially, that of the unification of different regions into one single nation. We hear overtones of Lavisse in Renan's assertion: "In the enterprise that the king of France, in part by his tyranny, in party by his justice, so admirably concluded, many other countries have failed at."[69] The "spiritual" element at the basis of a national identity does not develop spontaneously, nor is it a product of chance. It is a human artifact. The nation takes root in the realm of the imagination, the "spiritual," not the material.

This "spiritual principle" relies on a "present consensus" that must be constantly renegotiated, "the daily plebiscite," as he calls it elsewhere in the speech. It follows logically that the historical narrative upon which this consensus hinges must *also* be constantly renegotiated. In his speech, Renan again calls upon the example of the French king:

> The king of France who is, if I might say, the ideal type of a secular crystallizer; the king of France, who created the most perfect national unity possible; the king of France, seen from too close up, has lost his prestige; the nation that he had formed cursed him, and today, it is only cultivated minds who know his value and what he did.[70]

The nation repudiated the king who laid the foundations for its own creation; the present consensus, that is after 1789, chose to largely erase that figure from the Pantheon of heroes, a project that proved all too successful, in Renan's view. Even those figures included within the category of "great figures" at one moment do not permanently enter into the immutable empyrean—the past is elastic and negotiable.

Renan posits here what other more recent scholars second: a national history is *invented*, not *discovered*. In *The Invention of Tradition*, Eric Hobsbawm writes:

> The element of invention is particularly clear here, since the history that became part of the fund of knowledge or the ideology of nation, state or movement is not what has actually been preserved but what has been selected, written, pictured, popularized and institutionalized by those whose function it is to do so.[71]

And, as Claire Andrieu reminds us, "The question then is not to know if history is instrumentalized, but how it is."[72]

If the memory of notable ancestors constitutes the identity of a nation, as Renan confirms, the selection of "the great" is debated as a function of present interests. This "instrumentalization" of the past can be affirmed in a more recent example: Andrieu cites the "pantheonizations" that mark the period after World War II. The great heroes of France (among them Voltaire and Rousseau) are honored by interment in the Pantheon, a monument in the Latin Quarter. It was established as a mausoleum during the Revolution, and, not surprisingly, the first figure inhumed there was the Revolutionary leader Mirabeau. After World War II, there was a campaign to include new heroes suitable to the new age. In the 1950s and 1960s, members of the Resistance such as Jean Moulin and Jean Monnet were offered places, and two female resisters were added in the 1990s. These pantheonizations promoted the narrative of a "resisting France" rather than a "collaborationist France" during World War II and made room for women in that company.[73]

This past, this historical narrative is a creation with certain strategic ends, shape-shifting to respond to the requirements of its age. What Lavisse and Renan identify as the "legacy" of the nation is, in fact, an "emplotting" whose aim is to create and maintain ideological cohesion. It is fashioned with strategic ends in mind and can change in response to the requirements of the moment. In Anne-Marie Thiesse's words, "national history is not a product of the regime of truth of scholarly history or of justice. It projects on the past concepts, *mentalités*, problems that belong to the present."[74] We are quite far from the realm of the sempiternal and immutable.

Renan points out that the nation, this "spiritual construction," embraces two movements: one toward the commemoration of an official history held in common, woven out of "the great figures," "the great events," and "glory." The other movement moves toward oblivion. The French of the late nineteenth century have forgotten their "Burgundian, Alain, Taifale or Visigoth" roots, as well as the horrors of Saint Bartholomew's Day and the thirteenth-century massacres in the South of France.

> Forgetting, and I would even say historical error, are an essential factor in the creation of a nation, and so for this reason progress in historical studies is often a danger for nationality. Historical investigation, in fact, shines a light on acts of violence that occurred at the origin of all political formations, even of those whose consequences were the most beneficent. Unity is always created brutally; the joining of the North of France to the South of France was the result of extermination and a continuous terror that lasted almost a century.[75]

What is interesting—and what Paul Ricoeur,[76] among others, has noted—is the fact that Renan has no need to describe the events of Saint Bartholomew's Day, when royal mercenaries and Catholic mobs massacred numbers of Huguenots in Paris in 1572 during the wars of religion, nor must he outline the depredations inflicted on the Midi or South of France during the campaigns to subdue it to royal authority in the thirteenth century. Renan needs to do no more than name these events because, in fact, they have *not* been forgotten, despite the fact they were supposed to be erased from the national memory. It is not a question of *forgetting*, in these cases, but of *amnesia, repression*, two very different animals that cannot be summoned without risk and peril.

Simone Weil takes issue with several key aspects of France's sacred history. She most importantly and globally resists the master narrative of progress and how it was instrumentalized in the treatment of the French Revolution. To enshrine progress in world historical development, one must separate the present from the past, to argue one's own age as an advance on what preceded. So doing creates a chasm between the past and present, she argues, "uproots" contemporaries from the treasures of the past and gives them a very thin soul within which to grow. This was exactly the mission of the Revolution, in her view—to create "a violent break with the past."[77] The narrative of progress leads to erasures of certain luminous moments in French history. For example, in 1209 during the Albigensian Crusade the townspeople of Béziers refused to hand over their "heretic" Cathar neighbors to the crusaders, an act that resulted in their own massacre.[78] Weil argues that such moments are ignored because they disrupt the prevalent narrative—an act of bravery and conscience, probably unique in French history, that predates the key events of French sacred history, could unravel the entire narrative.

This negligent erasure leads to other willed lacunae in the historical narrative, an amnesia that has poisoned the French comity at its root. Although Weil never addresses Renan's essay directly except to signal that she had read it and found it "mediocre,"[79] her later writings on nation and history from the late 1930s and early 1940s clearly argue against Renan's theories.

Weil drew up a long list of events that Renan would doubtless suggest were better left to oblivion: she, too, brings up "territories situated south of the Loire"[80] (the Midi) and piles onto that the regions of Burgundy, Brittany, Franche Comté, and Corsica.[81] Like Renan, she emphasizes the "terror" and "brutality" inflicted upon those populations conquered by the French kings.[82]

But if Renan suggested that the commemoration of these events poses a danger to national unity, that they are better left as material for scholars, that to make them available to a national public threatens the present consensus, Weil draws the opposite conclusion: in her view, the danger resides, rather, in obscuring and forgetting.

One might well have forgotten Visigoth or Frankish ancestry, she concedes, but not whether one is a Provençal, Breton, or Corsican. Why, she asks, even in the 1930s, do a large number of Parisian prostitutes and illiterate soldiers come from Brittany, a province whose inhabitants proved so recalcitrant to forced "Frenchification" even through the nineteenth century? Why were Provençaux, the survivors of the brutal annexation to France and of the Crusades against their religious "heresies" in the thirteenth century, so well represented in the rabidly anticlerical Radical Party during the Third Republic? Why did Corsica supply so many police prefects, informers, and policemen if not to inflict on others what they themselves had suffered? For these populations with origins in territories brutally annexed to France, present-day ills can be traced to a repressed past, in Weil's view.[83]

Narrative psychology is helpful here in unspooling the components of this repression and its effects. If a master narrative can function to order a life story, to give it a familiar structure recognizable to a community, it can also operate for an opposite purpose. If an individual or a smaller group's narrative is not coherent in the eyes of those who hold to the master narrative, if acknowledgment is withheld, damage ensues to the outlier. Julie Beck's question is to the point: "So what to do, then, with all the things that don't fit tidily?" Robyn Fivush poses the dilemma succinctly:

> Narratives that are not coherent, that cannot be linked to meaningful explanations, can lead to identity confusion and fragmentation; this is often what happens following traumatic experiences that are silenced, both by the culture and by the individual, and cannot be integrated into a coherent sense of narrative and identity.... The individual must have a community of listeners able and willing to hear and validate their experiences in order to create more coherent narratives.[84]

Weil argues just this point—that those French populations whose traumatic experiences have been silenced, who find no larger community willing to hear and acknowledge them, fall into greater incoherence (Breton criminality, Corsican low-level oppression) and increasing marginalization. Incapable of ordering and recounting their past, they eventually forget and lose it, but do not for all that move beyond the trauma—it just burrows more deeply, operative but inaccessible to them. Narrative psychologists see warning signs in narrative incoherence: "Worry when your characters are not making sense and have them worry, too."[85]

Weil saw clearly that there is a point beyond which the official history "emprisons" rather than "structures," no longer offers an identity but deprives people of the possibility of knowing themselves and expressing this self. In the words of Paul Ricoeur:

> The major peril . . . is in the manipulation of history that is authorized, imposed, celebrated, commemorated—official history. The story, a resource, thus also becomes a trap when higher powers take over the direction of setting the plot and imposing a canonical story through intimidation or seduction, fear or flattery. A twisted form of oblivion is at work here, resulting from depriving social actors of their ordinary ability to recount themselves.[86]

In the examples adduced by Weil, we see the results of a forced forgetting, of a past blotted out in favor of another, official past, one that leads triumphally to the creation of the French nation and the Third Republic. A striking example of this celebration of erasure is to be found in Charles Bigot's *Le Petit Français*. He contemplates what would happen if the Lorraines, the Normans, the Bretons, and the Provençaux should persist, but "the Fatherland" were to disappear. "France" would no longer exist, in his view; in the place of a "nation," solid and compact, "nothing would be left but human dust."[87] Weil argues just the opposite, that dust was what was left when regional identities and cultures were blotted out: "The state is a cold thing that cannot be loved; but it kills and abolishes all that could be loved; so one is forced to love it, because that is all there is."[88]

So Simone Weil agrees with Lavisse and Renan on the outlines of this official history: that it valorizes the transformation of a collection of "conquered territories" into a "nation." This nation is founded on the assumption that "progress" entails the development of ever-larger political entities, the sacrifice of regional to more catholic identities, all accomplished through the use of force. However, while Lavisse and Renan saw this narrative as "admirably concluded," Weil repudiates it and takes it apart in her writings, as we shall see in more detail in what follows. The world had witnessed the logical closure to such a master narrative—the coming of Hitler represents the apotheosis of a history that valorizes ever-larger political entities created at the end of a sword.

This master narrative, this sacred history, shows serious fissures in the prewar years. The responsibility placed on it—to fashion a "citizen" of the French nation, of the French Republic, to ensure the "daily plebiscite" that granted it the right to govern—proved an increasingly impossible challenge. The searing defeat of 1940 added a significant "data point" that had to be incorporated into the master narrative and would of necessity realign it. In the best of cases, this realignment would constitute the "new result" that would reshuffle and order what had previously been a jumble. Or it could prove so disruptive as to make the entire edifice collapse.

The defeat of 1940 would require a re-emplotting of Republican sacred history. Would it threaten and scramble the consensus constructed in 1871 and the historical narrative that served as its "ideological cement"? Or would instead the "fluid situation" created by the Debacle ensure "new learning," prove "valuable" in uniting "old facts," posited by Ruthellen Josselson as another possible outcome of upheaval?[89] The next two chapters explore how this challenge was engaged.

NOTES

1. "Proclamer la République en France, *ça* les Français savent le faire, ils le font de temps en temps. En revanche, ils se sont montrés pendant un siècle incapables de la faire durer."

Mona Ozouf, "Jules Ferry," Lecture given at conference on Jules Ferry, Bibliothèque nationale, Paris, France, April 22, 2003. https://gallica.bnf.fr/ark:/12148/bpt6k1320764s?rk=21459;2.

2. Legitimists supported the claims of the house of Bourbon (Louis XVI's heir); Orleanists supported the house of Bourbon-Orléans (Louis Philippe's heir); Bonapartists supported the house of Bonaparte (Napoleon Bonaparte's heir).

3. Jean-Pierre Azéma and Michel Winock, *La IIIe République (1880–1940)*, 2nd ed. (Paris: Calmann-Lévy, 1976), 154.

4. Azéma, *La IIIe République*, 160.

5. "c'est dans sa séduction intellectuelle, les symboles qu'elle incarne, les idéaux qu'elle proclame, les ennemis qu'elle dénonce, c'est dans l'affection et la fidélité qu'elle a suscité à son endroit que la IIIe République a trouvé un solide principe de continuité."

Azéma, *La IIIe République*, 159.

6. "Pour aimer la France, il faut sentir qu'elle a un passé."

Simone Weil, *L'Enracinement, OC* V, Vol. 2 (Paris: Gallimard, 2013), 297.

7. Mark Philip Freeman, *Hindsight: The Promise and Peril of Looking Backward* (New York: Oxford University Press, 2010), 112.

8. Victor Schklovsky, *Theory of Prose* (Elmwood Park: Dalky Archive Press, 1990), 170.

9. Schklovsky, *Theory of Prose*, 206.

10. Northrop Frye, *Anatomy of Criticism*, First Princeton Paperback ed. (Princeton: Princeton University Press, 2000), 169.
11. Frye, *Anatomy of Criticism*, 169.
12. Hayden White, "Literary Theory and Historical Writing," in *The Content of the Form: Narrative Discourse and Historical Representation* (Baltimore: Johns Hopkins University Press, 1987), 8.
13. White, "Historical Emplotment and the Problem of Truth in Historical Representation," in *The Content of the Form*, 32.
14. White, *Metahistory: The Historical Imagination in Nineteenth-Century Europe* (Baltimore: Johns Hopkins University Press, 1973), 6.
15. White, *Metahistory*, 7.
16. White, *Metahistory*, 47.
17. White, *Metahistory*, 58.
18. White, *Metahistory*, 9.
19. Michael White, "Folk Psychology and Narrative Practice," in *The Handbook of Narrative and Psychotherapy: Practice, Theory and Research*, eds. Lynne E. Angus and John McLeod (Thousand Oaks, CA: Sage Publications, 2004), 38–39. https://search-ebscohost-com.ezproxyles.flo.org/login.aspx?direct=true&AuthType =cookie,ip&db=cat05473a&AN=les.1341780&site=eds-live&scope=site.
20. Kate McLean et al., "Identity Development in Cultural Context: The Role of Deviating from Master Narratives," *Journal of Personality* 86, no. 4 (August 2018): 633. doi: 10.1111/jopy.12341.
21. Robyn Fivush, "Speaking Silence: The Social Construction of Silence in Autobiographical and Cultural Narratives," *Memory* 18, no. 2 (2010): 89. doi: 10.1080/09658210903029404.
22. Maurice Halbwachs, *The Collective Memory*, 1st ed. Harper Colophon Books (New York: Harper & Row, 1980), 38.
23. Halbwachs, *The Collective Memory*, 51–52.
24. Freeman, *Hindsight*, 147.
25. Freeman, *Hindsight*, 112.
26. Freeman, *Hindsight*, 147.
27. Freeman, *Hindsight*, 110.
28. Julie Beck, "Life's Stories," *The Atlantic*, August 10, 2015. https://www.theatlantic.com/health/archive/2015/08/life-stories-narrative-psychology-redemption-mental-health/400796/.
29. Eugen Weber, *Peasants into Frenchmen: The Modernization of Rural France 1870–1914* (Stanford: Stanford University Press, 1976), 112.
30. Qtd. in Weber, *Peasants into Frenchman*, 111.
31. Qtd. in Weber, *Peasants into Frenchman*, 111.
32. Weber, *Peasants into Frenchman*, 308-9.
33. "Mes amis, les hommes de mon âge ont vu des choses terribles. J'ai vu, quand j'étais très jeune, au sortir du collège, j'ai vu le Deux-Décembre! J'ai vu des soldats égarés, soudoyés peut-être, fusiller sur les boulevard les républicains et jusqu'aux passants inoffensifs. J'ai vu des ouvriers, aveugles ou inconscients, ricaner sur le passage de l'Assemblée nationale qu'on menait à Maza."

Qtd. in Alfred Rambaud, *Jules Ferry* (Paris: Plon, 1903), 2.

34. Qtd. in Mona Ozouf, *Jules Ferry: La Liberté et la tradition* (Paris: Gallimard, 2014), 48.

35. Barry H. Bergen, "Primary Education in Third Republic France: Recent French Works," *History of Education Quarterly* 26, no. 2 (July 1, 1986): 276. doi: 10.2307/368743.

36. Alfred Rambaud, Minister of Public Instruction in his own right and supporter of Ferry's policies, offers the sweep of this years-long campaign to enact Republican education policies, including a number of moments in parliamentary debates between Jules Ferry, his supporters, and his many opponents in the chapter of his book on Ferry titled "L'Oeuvre scolaire" ("School Work").

37. Rambaud, *Ferry*, 110.

38. Pascal Dupuy, "The Revolution in History, Commemoration, and Memory," in *A Companion to the French Revolution*, ed. Patrick McPhee (Malden, MA: John Wiley & Sons, 2013), 487.

39. Ozouf, "Jules Ferry," Lecture.

40. Weber, *Peasants into Frenchman*, 333.

41. Antoine Prost, *Histoire de l'Enseignement en France 1800–1967* (Paris: Armand Colin, 1968). Jacques Ozouf and Mona Ozouf, *La République des instituteurs* (Paris: Gallimard-le Seuil, 1992).

42. Azéma, *La IIIe République*, 173.

43. "L'enseignement de l'histoire de France devait donc être le lieu de la mise en scène de l'unité nationale."

Jacques and Ozouf, *La République*, 367.

44. Weber, *Peasants into Frenchman*, 336.

45. Weber, *Peasants into Frenchman*, 334.

46. "il faut que le maître lui-même soit tout pénétré de ce qu'il enseigne. Il ne faut pas qu'il récite le soir ce qu'il a appris le matin."

Jean Jaurès, "Aux Instituteurs et Institutrices," in *Action socialiste: Première série* (Paris: Bellais, 1899), 18–19. https://gallica.bnf.fr/ark:/12148/bpt6k827450/.

47. "car c'est ma conviction profonde que le seul moyen de sauver la France est de donner aux jeunes Français des raisons précises d'aimer leur pays et leurs devoirs envers lui . . . Et la démocratie française sera enfin une réalité!"

Ernest Lavisse, "Lettres ouvertes aux instituteurs de France," in *Manuel général de l'instruction primaire: journal hebdomadaire des instituteurs*, 65e année, tome 34 (Paris: Hachette, 1898), 87. https://education.persee.fr/doc/magen_1257-5593_1898_num_65_34_32325.

48. "mais cent ans n'ont pas suffi pour faire pénétrer la liberté dans les âmes, ce que serait l'achèvement de la Révolution française. Vous le pouvez en donnant une attention particulière à l'instruction morale et physique."

Lavisse, "Lettres ouvertes aux instituteurs de France," 87.

49. "On montrera ensuite l'unification de la France par le progrès continu de l'autorité royale."

Lavisse, *Questions d'enseignement national* (Paris, Armand Colin, 1885), 191.

50. Lavisse praises those monarchs, for example Saint Louis IX, who imposed limits upon the depredations of the nobility and punished them for their mistreatment of the poor.
    Lavisse, *Histoire de France: Cours élémentaire*, 56ff.

51. Jean-Baptiste Colbert, Louis XIV's Comptroller-General of Finances, earns several pages of encomium for his tireless efforts to improve France's infrastructure.
    Lavisse, *Histoire de France: Cours élémentaire*, 114.

52. "C'est une indiscutable vérité que la Révolution française a fait un effort héroïque pour substituer à la monarchie ancienne le règne de la justice et de la raison . . . qu'elle a ouvert dans le monde une ère nouvelle, et que l'Europe presque tout entière a été comme refondue par elle."
    Lavisse, *Questions d'Enseignement national*, 194.

53. "La France veut que les petits Arabes soient aussi bien instruits que les petits Français. Cela prouve que notre France est bonne et généreuse pour les peuples qu'elle a soumis."
    Lavisse, *Histoire de France: Cours élémentaire*, 168.

54. Azéma and Winock, *La IIIe République*, 143.

55. "Définie comme l'acte de naissance de la vraie France, la Révolution devient l'observatoire privilégié à partir duquel on va juger . . . les événements et les personnages de l'histoire; après 1789, on approuve ce qui prolonge la Révolution; mais avant 1789, on cherche à découvrir tout ce qui l'annonce."
    Ozouf, "Manuels," 9.

56. "Si nous, socialistes français, nous étions indifférents à l'honneur, à la sécurité, à la prosperité de la France, ce ne serait pas seulement un crime contre la patrie que nous commettrions, mais un crime contre l'humanité, car la France, une France libre, grande et forte, est nécessaire à l'humanité. C'est en France que la démocratie est parvenue à sa forme la plus logique, la République; et, si la France baissait, la réaction monterait dans le monde. C'est en France, dans le pays de la Révolution, que le retour des tyrannies féodales ou cléricales est le plus difficile."
    Jean Jaurès, "La France et le socialism," in *Action socialiste: Première série* (Paris: Bellais, 1899), 372–73.

57. "Les Allemands sont un peuple très orgueilleux. Ils cherchent toutes les occasions de nous faire du mal."
    Lavisse, *Histoire de France: Cours élémentaire*, 162.

58. "Généraux officiers, fantassins, cavaliers, aerostiers, tous savent leur métier. Si la France est attaquée, tous feront leur devoir. *La France est bien défendue.*"
    Lavisse, *Histoire de France: Cours élémentaire*, 162.

59. Charles Bigot, *Le Petit Français* (Paris: Eugène Weill and Georges Maurice, 1884), 173. https://gallica.bnf.fr/ark:/12148/bpt6k948679p.

60. "les taches noires"
    Bigot, *Le Petit Français*, 23.

61. "Il n'est pas de mère que n'aimât mieux voir son fils mort que déshonoré. Un jeune homme qui s'est soustrait au service militaire, un soldat qui a reculé devant son devoir, peuvent être aussi beaux et aussi riches qu'ils voudront: ils sont sans honneur

aux yeux des femmes et des jeunes filles. Si elles aiment l'uniforme militaire, c'est que pour elles uniforme est synonyme de courage."
Bigot, *Le Petit Français*, 70.

62. Henry Rousso, *The Vichy Syndrome*, trans. Arthur Goldhammer (Cambridge, Massachusetts: Harvard University Press, 1991), 114.

63. "Surtout on pose à l'histoire le problème de la constitution de la nation. Dans l'esprit d'un Lavisse, ou d'hommes d'Etat positivistes comme H. Ferry ou P. Bert, c'était un choix délibéré, une tentative pour fonder une culte de la patrie dans lequel se réconcilièrent partisans et adversaires de la Révolution."
Prost, *Histoire de l'Enseignement en France*, 336.

64. Dominique Maingueneau, *Les Livres d'ecole de la République 1870–1914: discours et idéologie* (Paris: Le Sycomore, 1979), 10.

65. Ernest Renan, "Nouvelle Lettre à M. Strauss," in *La Reforme Intellectuelle et morale*, 3rd ed. (Paris: Michel Lévy, Freres, 1872).

66. "Rien de matériel n'y suffit. Une nation est un principe spirituel, résultant des complications profondes de l'histoire, une famille spirituelle, non un groupe déterminé par la configuration du sol."
Ernest Renan, *Qu'est-ce qu'une nation?*, Conférence faite en Sorbonne, le 11 mars 1882. 2. éd. (Paris: Calmann-Lévy, 1882), 25. https://fr.wikisource.org/wiki/Qu%E2%80%99est-ce_qu%E2%80%99une_nation_%3F.

67. "Deux choses qui, à vrai dire, n'en font qu'une, constituent cette âme, ce principe spirituel. L'une est dans le passé, l'autre dans le présent. L'une est la possession en commun d'un riche legs de souvenirs; l'autre est le consentement actuel, le désir de vivre ensemble, la volonté de continuer à faire valoir l'héritage qu'on a reçu indivis."
Renan, *Qu'est-ce qu'une nation?*, 26.

68. "Un passé héroïque, des grands hommes, de la gloire (j'entends de la véritable), voilà le capital social sur lequel on assied une idée nationale."
Renan, *Qu'est-ce qu'une nation?*, 26.

69. "Dans l'entreprise que le roi de France, en partie par sa tyrannie, en partie par sa justice, a si admirablement menée à terme, beaucoup de pays ont échoué."
Renan, *Qu'est-ce qu'une nation?*, 8.

70. "Le roi de France, qui est, si j'ose le dire, le type idéal d'un cristallisateur séculaire; le roi de France, qui a fait la plus parfaite unité nationale qu'il y ait; le roi de France, vu de trop près, a perdu son prestige; la nation qu'il avait formée l'a maudit, et, aujourd'hui, il n'y a que les esprits cultivés qui sachent ce qu'il valait et ce qu'il a fait."
Renan, *Qu'est-ce qu'une nation?*, 8.

71. Eric Hobsbawn, "Introduction, Inventing Traditions," in *The Invention of Tradition*, eds. E. J. Hobsbawm and T. O. Ranger (Cambridge: Cambridge University Press, 2012), 13.

72. "La question n'est donc pas de savoir si l'histoire est instrumentalisée, mais comment elle l'est."
Claire Andrieu, "Introduction: le pouvoir central en France et ses usages du passé, de 1970 à nos jours," in *Politiques du passé: Usages politiques du passé*

dans la France contemporaine, eds. Claire Andrieu, Marie-Claire Lavabre, Danielle Tartakowsky (Aix: Université de Provence, 2006), 16.

73. Andrieu, "Introduction," 21.

74. "L'histoire nationale ne relève pas du régime de vérité de l'histoire savante ou de la justice. Elle projette sur le passé des conceptions, des mentalités, des problèmes qui appartiennent au présent."

Thiesse, *Faire les Français*, 51.

75. "L'oubli, et je dirai même l'erreur historique, sont un facteur essentiel de la création d'une nation, et c'est ainsi que le progrès des études historiques est souvent pour la nationalité un danger. L'investigation historique, en effet, remet en lumière les faits de violence qui se sont passés à l'origine de toutes les formations politiques, même de celles dont les conséquences ont été le plus bienfaisantes. L'unité se fait toujours brutalement; la réunion de la France du Nord et de la France du Midi a été le résultat d'extermination et d'une terreur continuée pendant près d'un siècle."

Renan, "Qu'est-ce qu'une nation?," 7–8.

76. Paul Ricoeur, *La Mémoire, l'histoire, l'oubli* (Paris: Seuil, 2000), 576.

77. Simone Weil, *L'Enracinement, OC* V, Vol. 2 (Paris: Gallimard, 2013), 268.

78. Weil, *L'Enracinement*, 294.

79. Weil, *L'Enracinement*, 195.

80. "des territoires situés au sud de la Loire."

Weil, *L'Enracinement*, 198.

81. Weil, *L'Enracinement*, 198–200.

82. Weil, *L'Enracinement*, 197, 198.

83. Weil, *L'Enracinement*, 198–200.

84. Fivush, *Speaking Silence*, 96.

85. Jerome Bruner, "The Narrative Creation of Self," in *The Handbook of Narrative and Psychotherapy: Practice, Theory and Research*, eds. Lynne E. Angus and John McLeod, Counseling and Psychotherapy Transcripts, Client Narratives, and Reference Works (Thousand Oaks, CA: Sage Publications, 2004), 13. https://search-ebscohost-com.ezproxyles.flo.org/login.aspx?direct=true&AuthType=cookie,ip&db=cat05473a&AN=les.1341780&site=eds-live&scope=site.

86. "Le périle majeur . . . est dans le maniement de l'histoire autorisée, imposée, célébrée, commémorée—de l'histoire officielle. La resource du récit devient ainsi le piège, lorsque des puissances supérieures prennent la direction de cette mise en intrigue et imposent un récit canonique par la voie d'intimidation ou de séduction, de peur ou de flatterie. Une forme retorse d'oubli est à l'oeuvre ici, résultant de la dépossession des acteurs sociaux de leur pouvoir ordinaire de se raconter eux-mêmes."

Ricoeur, *La Mémoire*, 580.

87. "il ne resterait plus que de la poussière humaine."

Bigot, *Le Petit Français*, 13.

88. "L'état est une chose froide qui ne peut pas être aimée; mais il tue et abolit tout ce que pourrait l'être; ainsi on est forcé de l'aimer, parce qu'il n'y a que lui."

Weil, *L'Enracinement*, 204.

89. Ruthellen Josselson, "On Becoming the Narrator of One's Own Life," in *Healing Plots: The Narrative Basis of Psychotherapy*, The Narrative Study of Lives (Washington, DC: American Psychological Association, 2004), 124.

Chapter 2

The Double Challenge to "Sacred History"

Interwar Pacifism and the 150th Commemoration of the French Revolution in 1939

No monolithic consensus ever reigned on the Republican master narrative of French history. Those same groups and political parties that stood in resistance to the Republic in 1871—monarchists, the Catholic Church, and the revolutionary left—questioned its ideological underpinnings for its entire existence. And, in a cruel turn, the period after World War I saw resistance to that narrative grow among other, previously more supportive constituencies.

This chapter will explore two movements that called into question the validity of the Republican historical construct: the first is the pacifist movement that grew in response to World War I and was joined and even led by those strongest Republican proselytizers, teachers. The second is the commemoration of the 150th anniversary of the French Revolution in 1939, the *Centcinquantenaire*, which instead of celebrating and validating Republican sacred history became a battlefield for control of it.

The previous chapter laid out how central *revanchisme*, military revenge for the loss of Alsace and Lorraine, was to Republican history, and how pervasive it was in the school curriculum. World War I brought to tragic fulfillment the promise of a conflict to settle scores. The Germans, victorious and insolent in 1871 and in new possession of Alsace and Lorraine, met in their turn with the insolence and punitive armistice conditions of the victorious French in 1918 and were forced to cede those two provinces *back* to France.

The terms *patrie, pays,* and *nation*—fatherland, country, and nation—lose the blush of innocence after 1918, implicated as they were in the carnage of World War I. Simone Weil is one of a chorus of voices dissenting from the Republican brand of patriotism, which, as we saw, rested on both nationalism and militarism. It is important also to note that her teacher and intellectual mentor at Henri IV, Alain, was one of the strongest voices for pacifism in France in the interwar period.

In her 1938 article "Mise au point" ("A Closer Examination"), she notes that "France's name appears constantly in writing and speech. A country becomes a nation when it takes up arms against another country or gets ready to take them up."[1] And her skepticism is not aimed only at the terms used to designate France, but more fundamentally at the collectivity "France" itself.

Weil's leeriness took root within the context of the leftist political milieux active before 1938—unions, the pacifist movement, and the revolutionary left. The publications *La Revue pédagogique: L'École émancipée* (*The Pedagogical Review: The Liberated School*) and *La Révolution prolétarienne* (*The Proletarian Revolution*), to both of which Weil was a contributor, as well as the positions taken by absolute pacifists (*pacifistes intégraux*), who held that going to war even in self-defense was an unjustifiable taking of human life, suggest the range of responses to the Republican master narrative taken by the left, including, as stated above, from among some of its previously most ardent supporters, teachers. Significantly, many teachers refused to enroll in the military training offered to those pursuing higher education, the PMS (*Préparation militaire supérieure*), a program that would allow them to serve as officers while in the military. Obligatory at the *École normale supérieure*, in 1928 a majority of students signed a petition protesting the program.[2] *The Pedagogical Review: The Liberated School* was the official publication of the National Union of Teachers (*Syndicat national des instituteurs et des institutrices*), a union of primary school teachers, for the most part, affiliated with the *Confédération générale du travail* (CGT) (General Confederation of Labor). In its affirmation of the centrality of class struggle and its avowed aim to eradicate the distinctions between workers and owners, the CGT, and hence the National Union of Teachers, was left-wing and revolutionary. The editors of *The Proletarian Revolution* were syndicalist and communist. Before 1940, Weil's view of "France" was similar to that expressed by these groups and can effectively stand in for them.

The fact that Weil and others held such terms as "nation" and "fatherland" at arm's distance is understandable given the political discourse in France between the wars. None of the terms used to designate "France" was innocent: each implied a certain political stance and was freighted with meaning. The linguist Damon Mayaffre analyzed the speeches given by four politicians during the 1930s: André Tardieu, Étienne Flandin, Léon Blum, and Maurice Thorez. Tardieu and Flandin were representatives of the moderate right *Alliance républicaine démocrate* (Republican Democratic Alliance) and both served terms as France's prime minister; Léon Blum was the Socialist prime minister of the Popular Front government in 1936, which Maurice Thorez, the leader of the communist party, had been instrumental in assembling. Their differing choice of words to designate "France" is significant: the representatives of the right punctuate their addresses with "the land," "the fatherland," and "the earth."[3] These terms evoke a country coextensive with a territory with natural frontiers and, in Mayaffre's words, it's a quick trip "from territory to terrain, from terrain to the fertile, arable fields of sweet France."[4] The terms "soil" and "earth" suggest a France defined by a traditional rural economy and way of life, an identity that in the twentieth century was already belied by the growth of urban centers and the economies associated with them.

This conception of "France" suggests what would justify any entry into the war. In Tardieu's own words in 1933: "And then, suddenly, the land is threatened by an invader and there you have everyone responding: 'Present.'"[5] Only if there is a threat posed to the soil recognized as "France" is a war justified, and in that case *only* a defensive war. A war fought over more abstract principles could not in good faith be engaged, in Flandin's view, "against a presumed aggressor on the basis of a system of alliances much more complicated than those that existed pre-war."[6] The population most closely associated with "the earth"—the peasantry—suffered the most in World War I. It comprised three-fifth of the fighting effectives, mainly serving in the infantry, the branch that took the brunt of the losses, representing 55 percent of the dead or missing.[7] French leaders recognized this fact and wanted to avoid requiring again such sacrifices from a group so closely identified with "traditional" agrarian France. Even the Radical Party prime minister Daladier justified signing the craven Munich Agreement with Hitler in 1938 by saying he didn't want to sacrifice "another million or two million peasants."[8]

"Nation," the term that appears more frequently in the speeches of the politicians on the left, suggests, rather than any attachment to a rural past, that France established after the Revolution, with responsibilities to a wider liberty and Revolutionary values that do not respect frontiers. One only needs to note the initiatives taken by the Popular Front government of Léon Blum to come to the aide of Republican Spain in her fight against the Fascists in 1936 (initiatives that were eventually thwarted) to get an idea of the commitment toward expanding liberty beyond France's borders.

At such a moment, in such a political situation, it is understandable that one might hold all terms for "country" at arm's length given the fact that any choice might signal adherence to a specific politics or ideology.

But in some circles, a reluctance to choose between the terms "nation" and "French soil" goes further than a wish to avoid being stamped with a specific politics. For Weil and many others on the left, primacy is not granted to the collectivities "nation" or "country" during the 1930s. Despite her critique of aspects of Marxist thought (in, for instance, *Les Causes de la liberté et de l'oppression sociale* [*Oppression and Liberty*]), one can see the imprint of the Marxist left in her discussion of national identity.

For Weil pre-1940, a shared identity based upon economic class trumps that based upon nation, and for many reasons. In Marx's view, the nation does not represent any timeless entity. It is no more than an intermediate formation undergoing a process of disintegration, whose disappearance will clear the way for a broader collective identity. In addition, the proletariat draws no advantage from belonging to "a nation." In Marx's formulation in the *Communist Manifesto*, "the proletariat have no country,"[9] because in bourgeois society they are deprived of full participation in that collective. In the analysis of Maxime Rodinson, these convictions entail yet others: a devaluing of a nationalist ideology, which represents "the struggle of one nation for its total liberty, and its alone, with no considerations of other nations, and often for its power at the cost of other nations' liberty,"[10] and at the same time a valorization of class struggle, whose aim is "the abolition of classes, thus the suppression of privileges, the establishment of freedom and social equality."[11] Those who looked deeply into the order of things through a Marxist lens believed that speeding the dismemberment of the intermediary construct "the nation" would ultimately be to the interest of the working class.

In October of 1938, right after the Munich Agreement, which merely delayed the outbreak of war by conceding to Nazi Germany's claims to the Czech Sudetenland, *The Pedagogical Review*, the publication of the National Union of Teachers, laid out its reasons for supporting the accords.

> First of all, because this war will be waged for the exclusive profit of imperialisms, and we don't want to see people destroy each other for industrialists. We refuse to recognize nations and races: for us, all the workers of the world are our brothers, and the only frontiers that we know are those that separate the exploited from their exploiters, the international proletariat from global capitalism.[12]

The union espouses the principle of internationalism and so recognizes neither "race" nor "nation." In an article written in 1933 in response to the centenary of the birth of Paul Bert, deputy and Minister of Public Instruction after Jules Ferry's first term, Weil echoes the view held by her union and refutes all solidarity conferred by belonging to a nation. "And I search in vain for any reason whatsoever why I should cherish with less fraternal feelings my German comrades, known or unknown, than any random French person."[13]

On closer study, this transnational identity appears less "universal" than it might at first glance. The revolutionary left insists on the fact that the true divisions are not those between different *countries* but between different *classes* in the same country. Class interests trump nations' political interests. And if a transnational community exists among the classes, the left valorizes those links among the working classes alone.

Weil's pacifism, and that of others on the left, grows largely from this identification with the interests of the working class. In the view of revolutionary syndicalist movements, war serves as a weapon not between hostile nations but rather in the hands of the ruling class to maintain their power and crush the workers. This conviction is shared and expressed by the editorial committee of *The Pedagogical Review*, as cited above, and by Weil, writing in the review *La Critique sociale*, a publication with communist but anti-Stalinist sympathies founded by Weil's friend Boris Souvarine. Both share the conviction that every war constitutes "a fact of internal war" rather than "an episode of external war."[14]

And the results of such a war, for the nation which comes out victorious as for the one which meets defeat, are exactly the same for the workers: the consolidation of power into the hands of "the administrative, police and military apparatus . . . which calls itself our defender and turns us into its slaves,"[15] in Weil's wording. Her formulation resonates with the view of *The Proletarian Revolution* that a war results not in the liberation of subject peoples but in "the most degrading servitude."[16] Weil discounts the claims of any nation's "war aims." The interests of the transnational working class have priority. "It is necessary to look for what outcome would be the most favorable for the international proletariat and take sides accordingly,"[17] she writes.

She and her colleagues on the syndicalist left thus reject a national in favor of transnational identity and in fact associate any national sentiment with the propagandistic patriotism taught in the Republican schools. Weil quotes disdainfully the preface Paul Bert, the Minister of Public Instruction of the early Republic and one of the architects of the educational system, wrote for a book titled *Love of the Fatherland* (*Amour de la patrie*):

> *Civic education is the School's primordial function, the real raison d'être of the law for obligatory education,* the principal justification for the immense sacrifices which are imposed on the Nation for the instruction of her children, her future citizens, *her future defenders* [emphases in original].[18]

She characterizes this instruction in patriotism, which we saw laid out in Lavisse's histories and Bigot's manual on patriotism, as "brainwashing"[19] (*"bourrage de crane"*) which has one sole aim—the formation of future defenders of French soil. She rejects patriotism out of hand as "radically inhuman," good only for "transforming men into cannon fodder."[20]

This charge is brought by a large number of teachers after the Great War, particularly the members of the National Union of Teachers, to which Weil belonged, as we noted. Textbooks written directly after 1919, such as *Little French Children, Don't Forget! (Petits Français, n'oubliez pas!)*, instilled a patriotism intent on revenge, where the "simple soldiers" (*poilus*) figured as brave defenders of a triumphant France and the Germans as barbarians alone responsible for the war. Almost no mention was made of the number of victims, the trenches, shell shock, or civilian losses.[21]

Even before 1914 and the devastating losses of the war, there was a perceptible countercurrent to this militarism among teachers. The Ozoufs's *Republic of Teachers (La République des instituteurs)* is based on an extensive questionnaire sent out in 1961 to those who had taught between 1871 and 1914, after the founding of the Republic but before the outbreak of World War I. This generation represents the vanguard of the teacher-proselytizers, for the most part fully committed to the Republic, which represented "the framework and horizon of their thought,"[22] in the Ozoufs's formulation. Several of the respondents note that even before the Great War the tide had begun to turn against the blatant *revanchisme* as represented by Bigot's manual.[23] An indication that the teaching corps leaned against militarism is the fact that when asked what public personage they held in greatest esteem, an overwhelming majority named Jean Jaurès,[24] the leader of the French Socialist Party who spoke and agitated against the war until the last hour and was so clearly identified with the anti-war party that he was assassinated by a pro-war nationalist just days before war was declared.

Mona Siegel in *The Moral Disarmament of France*, her rich treatment of interwar education and its impact on pacifism, demonstrates that between 1925 and 1939 teachers and their unions were largely responsible for the revision of textbooks and a muting of their revenge patriotism. "Once marshaled to venerate French heroes, dehumanize the German army, and celebrate the nation's victory camp, scholastic narratives of the Great War became, from the mid 1920s to the late 1930s, eloquent testimonials to unprecedented human suffering and physical devastation."[25] In new and revised textbooks, the Germans no longer figure as the barbarian aggressors; they form, instead, a fraternity of suffering with French soldiers. The book *History of France (Histoire de France)* by Besseige and Lyonnais (1936), which Siegel adduces as an example, includes an etching to illustrate the Battle of Verdun. It depicts a pile of dead soldiers, their mouths agape in the rictus of their last moments, with the following caption: "This drawing, based on sketch done on site in 1916, at Fleury, after the taking of a trench, gives you an idea of what the tragic battle of Verdun was like."[26] During these years between the two wars, at least in the textbooks adopted by most of the unionized teachers, love for the fatherland includes pity for shared suffering and losses.

Antimilitarism, even pacifism, is espoused between the two wars by that other most important of interest groups, veterans of World War I, many of whom were also teachers. Even among veterans' groups on the right, the exaltation of military valor and glory ceded to a focus on "suffering, misery, mourning,"[27] in the words of Antoine Prost. In patriotic celebrations, notably the 14th of July, disabled veterans (*mutilés de guerre*) appeared at the head of all military parades, a reminder of war's horrific effects on the soldier.[28] Prost cites an article that appeared in November 1921 in a veterans' publication *Le Bequillard meusien (The Cripple (Crutch User) from the Meuse)*: "They must insist upon the horror of an evening after the battle: the dead, with their terrible grimaces, their gaping wounds, the shattered skull, entrails hanging ... the fetid stink that hangs over the mass grave."[29] The duty for passing on these lessons falls to "the teacher and the priest," in the view of the writer, because the true audience of this pacifist message is children.

Many of the numerous veteran groups came to see their erstwhile enemies, the Germans, as brothers in suffering and blamed the war on the emperor's imperialist ambitions rather than on the German people as a whole.[30] In addition, once Alsace and Lorraine were restored to France by the terms of the Treaty of Versailles, a thorny bone of contention that fed French hostility was removed.[31] It was possible to be a French patriot but share fellow feelings with a larger comity—humanity.[32]

This rejection of "classical" patriotism and nationalism serves as a foundation for certain forms of pacifism in the interwar period and feeds into it.

Before the Debacle, Weil espoused an integral pacifism, a pacifism in the new style, represented by the *Ligue internationale des combattants de la paix (LICP)* (International League of Fighters for Peace) as well as the editorial committees for the reviews *The Proletarian Revolution* and *The Pedagogical Review*. Integral pacifism "refused on principle all wars, and prefers servitude to war."[33] Pacifism in the new style faulted the unjust terms of the Treaty of Versailles which it judged responsible for the political impasse with Nazi Germany. In an article in *The Proletarian Revolution* titled "The Sudeten Question" ("La Question des Sudètes"), Robert Louzon, the journal's editor, reminds his readers that one of the aims of the victors in the Great War was to assure that "the German populations left outside of the 1871 unification not join it."[34] To this end, the Allies vetoed the 1919 Austrian plebiscite to unite with Germany, refusing the Austrians that right to self-determination enshrined as a principle in the Treaty of Versailles. Louzon underscores the injustice of this response and insists upon the fact that the Anschluss of 6 million Austrian Germans in March 1938 and the 3 million Germans in Bohemia in October 1938 does no more than rectify an historical injustice.[35]

This focus on a population's right to self-determination blunts the author's recognition of the harm done to Czechoslovakia by this amputation. The industries lost through the annexation include no more than the glass and ceramic works, he assures the reader, which will not materially weaken the economic base. There still remains "the essential"—"arable land, the flatlands, coal, Skoda," "the bases necessary to maintain an independent economy."[36] This same insensibility is discernible in Weil's pronouncements on the crisis. In the article "L'Europe en guerre pour la Tchécoslovaquie" ("Europe at War for Czechoslovakia"), first published in *Feuilles libres de la quinzaine (Free Sheets of the Fortnight)* (with pacifist, leftist but anti-communist leanings), she writes, "Czechs can proscribe the communist party and exclude Jews from unimportant positions without losing anything whatsoever of their national life."[37] This conviction that the annexation of the Sudetenland helped right a wrong enabled her absolute pacifist position and fostered a jarring insensibility to Czechoslovakian claims.

This pacifism in the new style draws from an alternative reading of the historical narrative to that propagated by revenge and militaristic propaganda. It presents the French pacifist movement not as hijacking sacred history but rather as revealing what has been in Republican DNA since its birth in the French Revolution.

In an article in *The Proletarian Revolution*, Georges Michon, an historian and author of *Robespierre and the Revolutionary War 1791–1792 (Robespierre et la guerre révolutionnaire 1791–1792)*, lays out his theory that modern French pacifism can be traced back to the Robespierre of 1791–1792 and his adamant resistance to war. This "great ancestor" was unwilling to drag a new nation into an enterprise that could endanger the political and social advances already achieved but as yet still fragile. The Robespierre portrayed by Michon is one who saw all too clearly that a war would serve not the Revolution but the Counter-Revolution.[38] Robespierre expresses his reservations in a speech given in January of 1792:

> The most extravagant idea that can arise in a politician's mind is to believe that it suffices that a people through force of arms enter among a foreign people to make them adopt their own laws and constitution. No one likes armed missionaries. . . . Before the effects of our revolution can make themselves felt in foreign nations, it has to be consolidated.[39]

Weil's analysis in "Réflexions sur la guerre" ("Reflections on the War") recalls that of Robespierre and underscores his clairvoyance.

> The goal of their [the *grands ancêtres*] existence was not to seize power but to establish an effective democracy, both democratic and social. It is a bloody irony of history that the war forced them to leave on paper the Constitution of 1793, to forge a centralized apparatus, to exercise a bloody terror that they could not even turn against the rich, to wipe out all liberty, and to make themselves

in short the quartermasters of Napoleon's military, bureaucratic, bourgeois despotism.[40]

The leftist, syndicalist, and pacifist press in France from 1938 to 1939 staged a frontal assault on the militaristic, nationalistic elements in French sacred history. A particularly effective avenue of attack, given the approaching celebration of the 150th anniversary of the French Revolution, is their argument that the Revolution, that keystone to Third Republic history, had been sidetracked and denatured by the Revolutionary Wars, not defined by them. The wars meant that a Revolutionary constitution had been left on the drafting table, that all attention was hijacked into waging wars rather than shoring up the social and political gains that had up to then been achieved. In this searing critique, they suggest that the initiating event of Third Republic history, the Revolution, was stillborn, and that in lionizing it the Republic is engaged in a malicious misreading of the intentions of that most grand of all *grands ancêtres*, Robespierre. Far from leaping joyously into wars that assured France's frontiers and expanded the "good news" of liberty abroad, Robespierre entered the war only reluctantly, understanding its ultimate cost to Revolutionary ideals. The "absolute pacifists" fire the first warning shots across the bow of the 150th commemoration of the Revolution.

To the same degree that the founders of the Republic realized the centrality of education to the national enterprise, they recognized as well that festivals and ceremonies could extend the reach of civic education, could marshal "symbols" to reinforce those lessons. The political theorist Karl Deutsch characterizes the "late stages of the nation-building process" as particularly adept at and dependent upon instrumentalizing the symbols of nationhood. "Anthems, flags and flag salutes" seep into and imprint themselves on a population through "informal group pressure," mass communication, and "all the coercive powers of the state."[41] Halbwachs's concepts of collective and social memory further illuminate how official commemoration functions to coalesce a group. A populace's scattered attention can be focused by calling to mind a significant past event. Even if it occurred far earlier, it can be "summoned," and responses to it can be evoked and "managed" by a present-day context that explicates it for a contemporary audience. Patrick Hutton characterizes Halbwach's analysis of commemoration in these terms:

> Commemorative places of memory reinforce our habits of mind by prompting our specific recollections of the past. That is why commemoration is so politically significant. As an activity it seeks to strengthen places of memory, enabling fading habits of mind to be reaffirmed and specific images to be retrieved more easily.[42]

Here Hutton hones in on two of Halbwach's key concepts: the reaffirmation of "habits of mind" through repetition and habituation and the political use value of such recall.

Mona Ozouf's study of the festivals instituted during the Revolutionary period makes a case for their power not only to evoke a narrative memory but tap into and channel a sense of the sacred. The *grands ancêtres* might have discouraged or prohibited the numerous Church feast days that cluttered the liturgical calendar, but they realized how useful a transfer of devotion from the church to the "nation" would prove. "Symbols, language and ritual" all would provide fungible tools and would enable a "transfer of sacrality onto political and social values,"[43] in Lynn Hunt's words. Halbwachs argues something similar, in Hutton's view:

> The events of the past that has grown distant and strange are thereby integrated into more familiar surroundings of the present. In this eclipse of time, memory builds an emotional link to the past rather than a critical perspective of it.[44]

Even if Hutton adopts the term "emotional" rather than "sacral," the contrast to "critical" remains at the heart of both formulations.

Central to the "sacralizing" of the Third Republic historical narrative is the celebration of Bastille Day, the 14th of July, 1789, which marked the first forceful mass uprising of the people of Paris against the perceived injustices of the monarchy. A crowd of approximately 1,000 Parisians, fearful that the arms stored in the prison citadel the Bastille were to be seized by the royal troops and used against them, stormed the fortress, killing its governor and 5 defenders. In the aftermath, the government agreed to remove those royal troops gathered in Paris and entrust the city's defense to the National Guard, a popular militia, which constituted a significant concession to the populace's demands. The success of this undertaking gave hope that royal authority could in fact be challenged and replaced.

The monarchist, restoration regimes of the nineteenth century created a *cordon sanitaire* around the Revolution in order to ensure their own legitimacy. And while the officials of the Second Republic celebrated the Revolution, they were chary of highlighting its more violent episodes: they chose as the national holiday May 4, the day of the opening of the Estates General in 1789.

The Third Republic, in contrast, cast the Revolution and the First Republic of 1792 as the keystone to its legitimacy, declaring a direct descendance from both. And they chose Bastille Day as the national holiday. In addition, they adopted as the national anthem the Marseillaise, a marching song chanted by volunteers from Marseille as they gathered in Paris to battle the foreign armies of the Coalition. They did not shy away from commemorating the popular violence of some of the Revolution's key events, nor the armed defense of the fatherland against invaders.

This link back to the Revolution was codified during the first years of the Republic and reinforced through the centennial celebration in 1889. Instituted as a national holiday by the new government and celebrated annually from 1889 on, it was the highest holy day in the Republic's sacred calendar. As Brenda Nelms notes, a sense of urgency pervaded both the commemoration of the centennial in 1889 and the 150th celebration in 1939, when an embattled Republic asserted its viability in the face of threats from the right.[45] The Revolution militant was wielded as a shield and weapon against concrete threats to the Republic, posed in 1889 Georges Ernest Boulanger and his followers. Boulanger, a popular military figure, was appointed Minister of War and drew mass support through his single-minded maneuvering to engage France in another conflict with Germany to the end of regaining the lost provinces of Alsace and Lorraine. His political movement, whose slogan was "Revanchisme, Révision, Restauration" (Revenge, Revision [of the constitution], Restoration [of the monarchy]), gained a good number of seats in the elections of 1888, and in January of 1889 he routed his opponent in the elections for deputy representing Paris. Those in government feared he would use this show of strength to stage a coup d'état and establish a military dictatorship. His delay in taking action gave the government time to counter any possible moves and put out a warrant for his arrest. He fled France and, a discredited man, committed suicide in 1891. But the young Republic felt as if it had survived this challenge by the skin of its teeth. The planners of the centennial had this recent menace clearly in mind: as one committee member planning commemorative events in Lyon expressed it, "Our true reason for glorifying the Revolution is that we still have before us the Counter-Revolution."[46]

The following words, taken from a speech by Senator Jean Macé at another planning meeting, constitute the closest approximation to an official governmental view of the centennial celebration, and thus of the Revolution itself:

> The date 1789 recalls the abolition of the private feudal structure which, with its abuses, its iniquities, its miseries, had survived the political feudal regime; the division of the provinces into departments; the organization of a new system of taxation based on individual quality . . . ; the beginnings of a complete system of national education . . . ; the abolition . . . in the family of privileges based on primogeniture; the suppression of classes; the division of property; the freeing of labor from its degrading status and its recognition as the source of all wealth, all strength for the state and all honor for the citizen; the proclamation of the rights of man and citizen which now form the charter of all free nations; finally, the French nation itself, risen from the ruins of the old regime and manifested in

the aspirations of its sons to live in peace and freedom, less for their own glory than for the honor and well-being of mankind.[47]

This passage offers a succinct exposition of the values of the new Republic; those who defend the Republic see an attack on the Revolution as tantamount to an attack on it and its version of "sacred history."

The French Revolution was as contested an event at its 150th commemoration as it was in 1889 at its centenary. In 1889, the new Republic and its stability were in question, threatened by internal dissent; in 1939, despite the fact the Republic was an established "fact," it was under threat from both internal political divisions and the external drumbeat of war. Joan Tumblety characterizes the situation in this mild formulation: "The Third Republic had not achieved total historiographical hegemony by the time the sesquicentenary of the revolution was celebrated in 1939."[48] The commemoration raised what François Furet termed "the fear of origins" ("la hantise des origines") and required a scrutiny of France's "true origin" ("l'origine vraie").[49] It called on the French to reflect on their shared national past and reconsider their national identity. The 1939 commemoration required that they face a fraught present and an unsettling future.

A wide range of studies were published in 1939 to mark the 150th anniversary, written by historians, politicians, and authors of more popular works. Throughout the jubilee year, newspapers and magazines dedicated articles as well as entire issues to the Revolution. The government and political parties tried to prime the pump of enthusiasm and reflection through a series of public pageants, exhibitions, and speeches. This chapter will consider a range of these texts and spectacles to discern the "official story" being recounted in a more than trying time, to recreate the mirror they held up to the French citizen. The year 1939 offered the opportunity to affirm French unity around a celebratory event; instead, it showed up the cracks threatening that unity: each party, each sector presented and celebrated *their own* rather than a common Revolution. What all these various commemorations shared, however, was the fact that, despite their divergent political views, they each mapped the preoccupations of 1939 onto the events of 1789.

The Fascist right, represented by *Je Suis Partout* (*I Am Everywhere*) and its collaborators, sits at one extreme of the continuum. This weekly publication kept up a concerted campaign against the Revolution and its commemoration throughout all of 1939 in articles written by its regular contributors Pierre Gaxotte and Lucien Rebatet and its editor Robert Brasillach.

An attack against the Revolution, that keystone event in the "sacred history" of the Third Republic, constitutes a strike against the Republic itself. Clemenceau's affirmation that "the Revolution is a block,"[50] that it's impossible to separate out its excesses and positive legacy, serves as a jumping-off point for journalists on the far right. They focus with grim jubilation on its excesses and use them as a sledgehammer to try to bring down the entire edifice. In his article "Les deux moteurs de la Révolution: Guerre et Inflation" ("The Two Motors of the Revolution: War and Inflation"), Gaxotte selects only the most grotesque revolutionary elements: "The Revolution without massacres, without guillotine, without proscription, without pillaging, without denunciations, without dictator, without prison, without assignats [bills issued as currency by the Revolutionary government], that's not the Revolution anymore."[51] For him and others, the Revolution is coextensive with its excesses.

And to desacralize the Revolution, this group attempts to undermine its foundations, prime among them is its *grands ancêtres*. Gaxotte dismisses them as a group of "absurd noblemen, deficient enlighteners, mediocre swindlers,"[52] in short, inept and middling figures. He reminds his readers that Billaud-Varenne, a Montagnard deputy at the National Convention and member of the Committee of Public Safety, so mistreated the slaves on his plantation in Cayenne that he could not sell them.[53] Robert de Brasillach presses the point that in 1789, Danton "didn't have a penny"[54] but ended up very rich.

They are painted as not merely ineffectual but also corrupt. Brasillach details the foundering of *la Companie des Indes* (French East India Company) during the Revolution and in the process implicates many of the *grands ancêtres* in that catastrophe. He then makes a swift swivel to the present and the scandals of the Third Republic and its personnel. "Our masters today, our Dantons, our Chabots, our Fabre d'Églantines, should consider that after our influence peddling . . . our speculations, our sell-outs, our scandals . . . they will end up by causing the Republic to fail."[55] If these writers keep one eye on the Revolution, the other is implacably fixed on the present.

And corruption is not the least of the failings of the *grands ancêtres*, in the view of *Je Suis Partout*. Even more serious is the charge that the men of 1792 instigated a war to solidify the Revolution. To distract the people from a foundering undertaking, they conjured up an outside enemy: "War was necessary."[56] This publication and those for whom it speaks accuse the Daladier government of taking a page from the Revolutionary playbook, of pushing France into an avoidable war to assure the survival of the Republic.

The views of the royalist right are represented by Daniel Halévy, an historian and polemicist who published his own take on the Revolution in 1939, titled *Histoire d'une histoire (History of a History)*, in an effort to offer a (royalist) critique of the works on the Revolution appearing in 1939. He terms Third Republic official history no more than a "legend," a "dogma,"[57] "a religious feeling"[58] whose "Koran" is the history textbooks available in primary, secondary, and university classrooms.[59] Halevy takes issue with the presentation of the Revolution in Third Republic historiography as an event that closes one age and launches a completely new one. In this construction, a "chasm" is formed between two different Frances, with all that precedes 1789 being swallowed by it (he shares this reservation with Simone Weil). He evokes admirable pre-1789 periods and institutions that have been buried in the rubble—the sixteenth century, that *grand siècle* of benevolence with its hospitals and other charitable foundations manned by the "saints and armies of charity."[60] If entire centuries are to be avoided, so are a whole class of words and concepts: "*God, faith, prayer* [emphasis in original], must not be spoken in front of the child, nor used by him."[61] Rather than a chasm between two Frances, Halévy prefers the metaphor of a "gap" (*écart*), "a wound that can heal."[62] He argues that a divided France is sick to the soul: "It's necessary to detach souls and attach them elsewhere: to convert them."[63] This mournful critique from the royalist right is a far cry from the rabid howls of the far right.

The right wasn't alone in attacking the Revolution and its legacy. The left did much the same in collections of historical documents, in monographs, in collections of articles and weeklies such as *Le Populaire*, the official newspaper of the Socialist Party, edited by Léon Blum.

The noted historian of the Revolution, Albert Saboul, in *1789: l'An un de la Liberté* (*1789: Year I of Liberty*), gathered a large number of historical documents and wrote a preface to frame them for the reader, bringing to bear a Marxist lens. He praises the energy of the bourgeois revolutionaries and criticizes the system they displaced as "an outdated ideology, an archaic and inefficient political system, propped up by a class of parasites."[64] In an afterward, he draws up a list of the permanent contributions brought by the Revolution:

> Individuals are no longer determined by the class they are born into, distinctions based on birth having been abolished; humans are born and remain free and equal in their rights; there can be no other difference between them except that resulting from their natural gifts and their usefulness to the common good.[65]

This enumeration of the advances effected by the Revolution continues for an entire page.

But the event does not escape all criticism. Soboul and others on the left characterize the Revolution as "bourgeois" because of the advantages it overwhelmingly conferred on this class to the detriment of the working class. The July 14, 1939, edition of *Le Populaire*, the Socialist daily, gives an account of this glorious day in 1789. The journalist reminds the reader that, despite some misgivings toward the events that transpired, despite the "innocent" victims it might have taken, violence was necessary.

> The people, risen up, put an end, in a few hours, to an oppression of ten centuries. Because it is the people who did it all. The bourgeoisie remained at the

Hôtel de Ville (City Hall), sparing of its blood and of its money, concerned exclusively with avoiding a fearsome conflict.[66]

The working class, despite the heroism they displayed, had gained fewer advantages by the end of the Revolution than the self-preserving bourgeoisie. And the present-day economic and political system carries forward the inequalities codified by the Revolution. In Soboul's view, it lay the foundation stone for the present, both what it contains of the good and of the bad. But, in the final analysis, these representatives of the left are also certain that it set a precedent for the future. "The Revolution, quickening its course, can prepare new tomorrows for anxious peoples."[67] Soboul, a member of the Communist Party, has his eyes fixed on a future where another, more pervasive shakeup will overturn a system that favors certain classes to the detriment of others.

In a selection of articles published in a special issue of the *Cahiers du Bolchévisme* (*Notebooks of Bolshevism*), the communist party emphasizes the centrality of those revolutionary events, even the bloodiest, where the working classes held central roles.

> During these years 1789–1794, during the course of which the frontiers were breached, the Jacobins thought that there was no salvation outside of contact with the popular masses. . . . *It is for this reason that they saved both France and democracy* [emphasis in original].[68]

The writer goes on to target the Daladier government, which, in his view, is taking an opposite and dangerous tack. "Today the following theory is developing: when the country is menaced, you don't give voice to the people, you put the parliament to sleep, you multiply the barriers to the right of assembly."[69] In April of 1938, President Daladier had sent up a bill that would grant the prime minister the authority to legislate by fiat and reduce the Assembly and Senate to a consultative role. Communist deputies had abstained from voting on this bill, understandably in view of the fact that one of the most controversial decrees which followed was the near nullification of the social legislation of the Popular Front concerning weekly work hours and the right to strike.

The representatives of the Communist party planned commemorations for the entire jubilee year in different parts of France. They dug into regional archives in order to demonstrate the support of the Revolution by local populations and to oppose the accounts that portrayed a Revolution initiated in the capital and imposed on resisting populations.[70]

Given this wide range of responses to the Revolution in 1939, often conflicting in their emphases, it fell to the government to take in hand the officially-sanctioned presentation and framing of the Revolution during this jubilee year. Edouard Herriot, former prime minister and serving president of the Chamber of Deputies, and Edouard Daladier, prime minister in 1939, are two of the most important spokesmen for this commemoration.

In a monograph written in 1939, *The Wellsprings of Liberty* (*Aux Sources de la liberté*), Herriot describes France as a direct heir of the Revolution, and the Revolution in turn as an heir of the Enlightenment. For him (and others) the origin of the Revolution can be traced back to the ideas of Rousseau, Voltaire, and Montesquieu, who figure in his text as the forefathers of the *grands ancêtres*.

Former prime minister Clémenceau had proclaimed once in the Senate, as mentioned above, that the Revolution is "a block," that it creates a whole, that unpleasant incidents cannot be removed in order to make it more palatable. Herriot refutes the claim. In his view, the terror and the murder of the king's guards in 1792 during the storming of the Tuileries were indeed horrific, but are outweighed by the advances the Revolution brought forth. He identifies the "true" Revolution with its nobler achievements—the rights granted to Jews and to people of color, the educational system, the citizens' army, and the rejection of wars of annexation. All these, despite the later military defeats of Napoleon and Louis Napoleon, are permanent gains. "Victorious even in defeat, the French won over to their ideas even those nations which had revolted against her domination."[71]

Herriot then turns to the present situation—the war which is breaking on the horizon at a moment of national disunity. He recalls for the reader August 4, 1789, when the Assembly voted for the abolition of feudal rights and privileges.

> There are no longer, that night, nobility, prelates, peasants. There are only Frenchmen and women. Brittany, Burgundy, Dauphiné, Provence renounce their orders. France from that point on must be no more than a large "family house," the deputies from Lorraine declare. In the fire of enthusiasm, national unity is achieved.[72]

This recall of that moment in 1789 is a clear exhortation to the French of 1939 to cease defining themselves by their differences but instead to hold to a common past, excised of its divisive excesses.

The benefits of the Revolution transcend France's frontiers, in Herriot's view, and more than just France must rise to defend them.

> At a moment when democratic principles are defied and mocked by the immorality of states termed totalitarian, what interests us . . . is to observe that a community like this uniting Great Britain, the United States and the French Republic

creates the deep and permanent reason for their necessary solidarity and their obligations toward a world which brutal codes of barbarity want to dominate.[73]

Great Britain is already an ally whom he wants to encourage. The United States, on the other hand, has not yet joined the fight, but given its historic stake in the legacy of the French Revolution, its natural place is at the side of the Allies. Here Herriot makes his case to several different audiences: his fellow citizens, France's Allies, and her future Allies. His exhortation encourages those who are already in the fight to carry on and those who are undecided to join it. "This dynamism of liberty—will it be exhausted?"[74] he asks at the end of his monograph. And in 1939, the answer was not at all clear.

The official ceremonies to mark this anniversary reveal clearly the government's hopes for the jubilee. Three signal moments were celebrated on three dates by three different ceremonies: May 5, the opening of the Estates General; July 14, Bastille Day; and August 4, the abolishment of feudal privileges; the second of these clearly being the most important.

The celebration on the 14th of July was similar to earlier ones in many regards: there were speeches, a military parade, numerous popular dances held in neighborhoods, and fireworks displays. In addition to these mainstays, there were spectacles that gathered representatives of different regions, for example, shepherds from Les Landes, singers from Metz, Lorraine, the Jura, and Arles. This gathering and showcasing of the traditions of different regions recalls the Festival of Federation (*Fête de la Fédération*) of 1790, which brought representatives from every corner of France to pledge fealty to the newly formed (and short-lived) constitutional monarchy in a visual display of French unity.

The entire range of the press, from anti-Republican papers such as *Je Suis Partout* and *Le Petit Parisien*, to those on the left such as *L'Humanité* and *Le Populaire*, were dazzled by the military parade. Marching along with the French troops was a large contingent of British soldiers—Coldstream Guards, Royal Guards, and Scots Guards—as well as troops representing France's far-flung empire, Algerians, Moroccans, Senegalese, and Indochinese. The inclusion of these military forces served to signal the links between France and her Allies and empire, of course, but even more importantly demonstrated the military force that was pledged to the fight should it come to France.

Daladier's short comments highlight France's military readiness. "This army that you cheered this morning is the guardian of your freedoms. You understood that it was capable of shattering any attack that could put our country in danger."[75] That the government hoped to highlight this strength is not surprising: the front-page headlines of many newspapers that same day featured the increasingly fraught situation in the Free City of Dantzig, contested by both Germany and Poland, as well as the economic agreement signed by Italian Foreign Minister Ciano and Franco, the Generalissimo of Fascist Spain. The Fascist vice was tightening.

Simone Weil engages the 1939 national discussion of the Revolution in articles such as "Réflexions en vue d'un bilan" ("Reflections in View of an Assessment") and "Quelques réflexions sur les origines de l'hitlérisme" ("The Great Beast: Reflections on the Origins of Hitlerism"), both written during the jubilee year. Without addressing the commemorative activities directly, these articles suggest how attentively she followed the debates around the meaning of the Revolution and how thoroughly she rejected its central thrust: the triumphal touting of France, the womb of liberty, which claimed for itself the role of "thinking for the universe."[76]

Her treatments are at cross-currents with those of most of her contemporaries and signal the beginning of a long project to disassemble French sacred history. First, she does not see the Revolution as the milestone event of modern France, but instead as a significant moment in a line of development within which it merely takes its place. Second, she rejects the triumphalism espoused by boosters of the Revolution: liberty is not the connecting thread in French history, far from it.

One passage from "The Great Beast" gathers many of Weil's objections to this triumphalist theme:

> One claims that Napoleon propagated, arms in hand, the ideas of liberty and equality of the French Revolution; but what he principally propagated is the idea of the centralized state. . . . The state thus conceived, invented, so to speak, by Richelieu, taken to a higher point of perfection by Louis XIV, to an even higher point by the Revolution, afterward by Napoleon, has found it supreme form today in Germany.[77]

This single paragraph is a tightly packed explosive put against the foundational beliefs of the Third Republic. If Herriot pushed the origin of the Revolution back 50 years to the Enlightenment, Weil pushes it back 100 years beyond that, to the reign of Richelieu. Rather than an origin, the Revolution takes its place in an already operative continuum: it advances what was in motion well beforehand.

And those who set the stage for this continuum of French history were not the "Enlightened." In the two articles written in the course of 1939, Weil does not even mention the name of a *grand ancêtre*, does not refer to any foundational revolutionary event, but instead has Napoleon stand in for the entire Revolution and bring it to its logical conclusion. Almost all mention of the word "Revolution" is absent from what she wrote in 1939, but Richelieu, Louis XIV, and Napoleon recur. These three figures constitute the real *grands ancêtres* of Weil's counternarrative.

Most shocking of all, the continuum that includes the Revolution does not find an apotheosis in the democracy celebrated in France in 1939, but in the Fascism imposed in Germany. This fact demonstrates the distance between her own version of French history and the Republican sacred history touted and celebrated throughout the entire jubilee year. Rather than a narrative that, in Pierre Azéma's words, builds upon "the taking of the Bastille, the night of August 4, the end of privileges, the coming to power of the people, the rising of the people against a coalition of despots,"[78] in Weil's version the coming to power of Richelieu leads to the Revolution which leads to Napoleon who leads to Hitler. And if Herriot can proclaim the Revolution's ultimate victory in the propagation of liberty under the Revolutionary and Napoleonic armies, Weil brings attention back to the fact that this was accomplished at sword's point. Weil transforms the triumphalist narrative celebrated by the parties of the center and left into an infernal machine. The mirror she offers up to the French reflects back to them a nightmare endpoint—the image of Hitler.

There are some resonances between her critical views on the Revolution and those of the right. They as well renounce the Revolution. But the causes for this repudiation differ. The right, for the most part, regrets the Revolution's abolition of the monarchy, but Weil sees little light between Richelieu, the monarchy's representative, and the Revolution: both extended and solidified the power of the state and both advanced a program of centralization. She transforms the narrative offered by the right by inserting Richelieu and the monarchy he served and strengthened into a thread that leads to the very Revolution the right repudiates. In addition, she puts distance between her own views and theirs when she voices regrets that some promising moments of French history that set the stage for the Revolution are completely absent in Republican sacred history—anything related to the emancipation of the serfs, revolts in the fourteenth century, Francois I's plans for a militia, "because the noblemen objected that if it were realized the grandsons of militiamen would be noblemen and their own grandsons would be serfs."[79] Her admiration for those moments in French history that proposed limits on aristocratic privilege clearly put her at odds with the forces of Counter-Revolution represented by the nobility.

In addition, Weil takes exception to the view shared by the Radical government and the left that France is a worldwide symbol of liberty.

> France must appear to its own citizens and the world as a perpetually gushing spring of freedom. There should not be even one person in the world sincerely loving freedom who might entertain legitimate reasons to hate France; all serious people who love liberty should be happy that France exists. We believe that's the case, but that's a mistake; it depends upon us to ensure in the future that it be true.[80]

The repetition of the verb "must" and "should" poses this image of France as a project, a moral imperative given to the French, not as something already accomplished by the Revolution. During this same period, Weil is also writing a number of articles on colonialism, and she understands only too well that there are those who have legitimate cause to "hate France."

In 1939 the government, by means of this jubilee, targets the present and the dangers that are forming on the horizon. The left, in contrast, is sketching out a future, perhaps in the near term, where the revolutionary project will be accomplished. That future will be mapped out on already-existing models offered by the French and Russian Revolutions and will constitute the "1917 of the people of France"[81] when human rights will include workers' rights.

As opposed to these views, Weil sees the French "project" not as having been achieved and as impossible to build on a preexisting model; it must yet be fashioned, with no model to build from, in the future, and only if the French accept the challenge to undertake it.

This moment constitutes a significant step in Weil's thought. Reflected in her articles during this period are the debates engaged in 1939 on "the French mission," on the ideals that France represents, and on its heroes. Clear as well is her unease in the face of the triumphalism at the heart of these discussions, empty, cheap affirmations, in her view. What we see in her writings in 1939 is the first draft of a response, not only to counter the Republican mental construct but to imagine a more ambitious and a truer one. Four years later, she will imagine a comprehensive alternate project for France in *L'Enracinement (The Need for Roots)* a work whose goal is no less than to "refashion the soul of a country."[82]

A transformation will be worked in the integral pacifist who couldn't support even defensive wars, in the radical syndicalist who found no reason why she should love any of her compatriots more than any citizen from another country.[83] She comes to fully repudiate these views as a "criminal offense against the fatherland,"[84] and what she would write during the war years constitutes a full-throated dirge for a beloved country and compatriots.

This jubilee year 1939 will see, as we know, the outbreak of war, which will end in France's capitulation to Germany, termed the Debacle, and years of Nazi occupation. After 1940, during the occupation, the debate on the French historical narrative will be taken up again in light of France's defeat at the hands of Fascist power. As the resistant Pierre-Jean Jouve would assert in 1944,

> The disaster of France in 1940 posed once again, in the clearest light, the question of the French Revolution. It wasn't possible to secure the capitulation of the nation . . . except by acting above all against the ideological patrimony of the Great Revolution.[85]

The adversarial parties, the battle lines, and the main points of the debate were already clearly drawn at this commemoration and will continue after the Debacle with even greater vehemence, as we will see in the next chapter.

NOTES

1. "le nom de la France revient sans cesse sous la plume et sur les lèvres. Un pays devient nation quand il prend les armes contre un autre ou s'apprête à les prendre."

    Simone Weil, "Mise au point," *OC* II, Vol. 3 (Paris: Gallimard, 1989), 97.

2. Julian Jackson, *The Fall of France: The Nazi Invasion of 1940* (New York: Oxford University Press, 2003), 148.

3. "le sol," "la patrie," "la terre"

    Damon Mayaffre, "'Nation' et 'Patrie' dans le discours de droite à la veille de la guerre: quels signifiants pour signifier quel patriotisme?" *Cahiers de lexicologie* 76, no. 1 (2000): 138, hal-0055387.

4. "du territoire à la terre, de la terre aux champs fertiles et labourables de la douce France."

    Mayaffre, "'Nation,'" 139.

5. "Et puis, tout d'un coup, le sol est menacé par l'envahisseur et voilà que tout le monde répond: 'Présent.'"

    Qtd. in Mayaffre, "Nation," 139.

6. "contre un agresseur présumé en vertu d'un système d'alliances beaucoup plus compliquées que les alliances d'avant-guerre."

    Qtd. in Mayaffre, "Nation," 139.

    As an example of how quickly one's views toward military engagement with Germany could change, Flandin, who as Foreign Minister had sought a strong riposte to the occupation of the Rhineland and who later supported the Franco-Soviet Pact, was a full-throated *munichois* in 1938 and hung posters up all around Paris before the accords were signed warning "People of France, you are being deceived! A cunning trap has been set . . . to make war inevitable."

    Qtd. in Jackson, *The Fall of France*, 113.

7. Gordon Wright, *Rural Revolution in France: The Peasantry in the Twentieth Century* (Stanford, CA: Stanford University Press, 1964), 29.

8. Qtd. in Gordon Wright, *Rural Revolution*, 28.

9. "les prolétaires n'ont pas de patrie."

    Karl Marx, *Communist Manifesto*, Marxists Internet Archive. https://www.marxists.org/archive/marx/works/download/pdf/Manifesto.pdf.

10. "la lutte d'une nation pour sa liberté globale à elle seule, sans considérations des autres et souvent pour sa puissance au détriment de la liberté des autres."

    Maxime Rodinson, "Le Marxisme et la nation," *L'Homme et la société* 7, no. 1 (1968): 148. https://www.persee.fr/doc/homso_0018-4306_1968_num_7_1_1104.

11. "l'abolition des classes, donc la suppression des privilèges, l'établissement de la liberté et de l'égalité sociale."

Rodinson, "Le Marxisme," 148.

12. "D'abord parce que cette guerre sera faite au profit exclusif des impérialismes et que nous ne voulons pas voir les peuples s'entredétruire pour les industriels. Nous nous refusons à connaître les nations et les races: pour nous, tous les travailleurs du monde sont des frères et les seules frontières que nous connaissons sont celles qui séparent les exploités de leurs exploiteurs, le prolétariat international du capitalisme mondial."

Gilbert Serret, "Tous debout contre la Guerre qui rôde," *Revue pédagogique: L'École émancipée* 21, no. 1 (October 2, 1938): 5.

13. "Et je cherche en vain une raison quelconque au nom de laquelle je devrais chérir moins fraternellement mes camarades allemands, connus ou inconnus, que n'importe quels Français."

Qtd. in Simone Pétrement, *La Vie de Simone Weil* 1 (Paris: Fayard, 1973), 341.

14. "un épisode de la guerre extérieure," "un fait de la guerre intérieure."

Simone Weil, "Réflexions sur la guerre," *OC* II, Vol. 1 (Paris: Gallimard, 1988), 293.

15. "l'appareil administratif, policier et militaire . . . celui qui se dit notre défenseur et fait de nous ses esclaves."

Weil, "Réflexions sur la guerre," 299.

16. "la servitude la plus dégradante"

M. Chambelland, "La Conférence de la Pentecôte: Bloc contre la guerre et l'union sacrée," *La Révolution prolétarienne* 14, no. 272 (June 10, 1938): 4–172. https://gallica.bnf.fr/ark:/12148/bpt6k6289927f/f2.item.

17. "Il faut . . . chercher quelle issue serait la plus favorable au prolétariat international, et prendre parti en conséquence."

Weil, "Réflexions sur la guerre," 289.

18. "*l'enseignement civique est la fonction primordiale de l'École, la vraie raison d'être de la loi d'obligation*, la justification principale des immenses sacrifices qui s'imposent à la Nation pour l'instruction de ses enfants, de ses futurs citoyens, *de ses futurs défenseurs*"

Simone Weil, "Le centenaire de Paul Bert," *OC* II, Vol. 1 (Paris: Gallimard, 1998), 233.

19. Weil, "Le centenaire de Paul Bert," 235.

20. "radicalement inhumain," "transformer les hommes en chair à canon."

Weil, "Le centenaire de Paul Bert," 235.

21. Mona L. Siegel, *The Moral Disarmament of France: Education, Pacifism and Patriotism, 1914–1940* (New York: Cambridge University Press, 2004), 69.

22. "cadre et horizon de leur pensée."

Jacques and Mona Ozouf, *La République des Instituteurs* (Paris: Gallimard-le Seuil, 1992), 148.

23. Ozouf, *République*, 137.

24. Ozouf, *République*, 164–67.

25. Siegel, *Moral Disarmament*, 152.

26. "Ce dessin, d'après un croquis pris sur place en 1916, à Fleury, après la prise d'une tranchée, vous donne une idée de ce que fut la tragique bataille de Verdun."

Qtd. in Siegel, *Moral Disarmamant*, 147.

27. Antoine Prost, *Les Anciens Combattants (1914–1939)* (Paris: Gallimard/Julliard, 1977), 101.

28. Prost, *Combattants*, 100.

29. "Ils doivent insister sur l'horreur d'un soir de bataille: les morts, avec leurs grimaces atroces, leurs blessures béantes, la tête fracassée, les entrailles pendantes . . . la fétide puanteur qui plane sur le charnier"
Qtd. in Prost, *Combattants*, 102.

30. Prost, *Combattants*, 86.

31. Prost, *Combattants*, 78.

32. Prost, *Combattants*, 83.

33. "refusait par principe toute guerre, et préfère la servitude à la guerre."
Gilbert Merlio, "Le Pacifisme en Allemagne et en France entre les deux guerres mondiales," *Les Cahiers Irice* 8, no. 2 (2011): 40. doi: 10.3917/lci.008.0039.

34. "les populations allemandes laissées en dehors de l'unité de 1871 ne viennent s'y joindre."
Robert Louzon, "La Question des Sudètes," *La Révolution prolétarienne*, no. 278 (September 10, 1938): 279–80. https://gallica.bnf.fr/ark:/12148/bpt6k62899335/f1.image.

35. Louzon, "La Question des Sudètes," 279.

36. "l'essentiel," " le sol arable, les plaines, le charbon, Skoda," "les bases nécessaires au maintien d'une économie indépendante."
Robert Louzon, "Tchécoslovaquie et France," *Révolution prolétarienne*, no. 280 (October 10, 1938): 307–308. https://gallica.bnf.fr/ark:/12148/bpt6k62899350.

37. "Les Tchèques peuvent interdire le parti communiste et exclure les Juifs des fonctions quelque peu importantes, sans perdre quoi que ce soit de leur vie nationale."
Weil, "L'Europe en guerre pour la Tchécoslovaquie?" *OC* II, Vol. 3 (Paris: Gallimard, 1989), 82.

38. Georges Michon, "Comment abattre le fascisme," *La Révolution prolétarienne*, no. 264 (February 10, 1938): 12–44. https://gallica.bnf.fr/ark:/12148/bpt6k6289919w?rk=64378;0.

39. "La plus extravagante idée qui puisse naître dans la tête d'un politique est de croire qu'il suffise à un peuple d'entrer à main armée chez un peuple étranger, pour lui faire adopter ses lois et sa constitution. Personne n'aime les missionnaires armés . . . Avant que les effets de notre révolution se fassent sentir chez les nations étrangères, il faut qu'elle soit consolidée."
Maximilien Robespierre, "Discours sur la guerre," prononcé à la Société des Amis de la Constitution, le 2 janvier 1792, an quatrième de la Révolution, *Discours par Maximilien Robespierre—5 Février 1791–11 Janvier 1792, Project Gutenberg*, https://www.gutenberg.org/files/29775/29775-h/29775-h.htm.

40. "Le but de leur existence n'était pas de s'emparer du pouvoir, mais d'établir une démocratie effective, à la fois démocratique et sociale. C'est par une sanglante ironie de l'histoire que la guerre les contraignît à laisser sur le papier la Constitution de

1793, à forger un appareil centralisé, à exercer une terreur sanglante qu'ils ne purent même pas tourner contre les riches, à anéantir toute liberté, et à se faire en somme les fourriers du despotisme militaire, bureaucratique et bourgeois de Napoléon."

Weil, "Reflexions sur la guerre," *OC* II, Vol. 1 (Paris: Gallimard, 1989), 294.

41. Karl W. Deutsch, "The Growth of Nations: Some Recurrent Patterns of Political and Social Integration," *World Politics* 5, no. 2 (January 1953): 189. doi: 10.2307/2008980.

42. Patrick H. Hutton, *History as an Art of Memory* (Lebanon, NH: University Press of New England, 1993), 79–80.

43. Lynn Hunt, "Forward," Mona Ozouf, *Festivals and the French Revolution* (Cambridge, MA: Harvard University Press, 1988), xii.

44. Hutton, *History*, 128.

45. Brenda Nelms, *The Third Republic and the Centennial of 1889* (New York: Garland, 1987), 10.

46. Qtd. in Nelms, *The Third Republic*, 144.

47. Qtd. in Nelms, *The Third Republic*, 198.

48. Joan Tumblety, "'Civil Wars of the Mind': The Commemoration of the 1798 Revolution in the Parisian Press of The Radical Right," *European History Quarterly* 30, no. 3 (July 2000): 391. https://search-ebscohost-com.ezproxyles.flo.org/login.aspx?direct=true&AuthType=cookie,ip&db=edb&AN=3435267&site=eds-live&scope=site.

Tumblety gives a thoroughgoing treatment of the responses of a wide range of right-wing movements and their publications in this article, from the Croix de feu (nationalist) to Action française (royalist) to the PPF (fascist).

49. François Furet, *Penser la Révolution française*, 2nd ed. (Paris: Gallimard, 1983), 14.

50. "la Révolution est un bloc."

Georges Clemenceau, Speech before the National Assembly, Jan. 29, 1981, Great Speeches, National Assembly website. https://www2.assemblee-nationale.fr/decouvrir-l-assemblee/histoire/grands-discours-parlementaires/georges-clemenceau-29-janvier-1891.

51. "La Révolution sans massacres, sans guillotine, sans proscription, sans pillages, sans dénunciation, sans dictateur, sans prisons, sans assignats, ce n'est plus la Révolution."

Pierre Gaxotte, "Les Deux Moteurs de la Revolution: Guerre et Inflation," *Je Suis Partout* 499 (June 30, 1939): 1. https://www.retronews.fr/journal/je-suis-partout/30-juin-1939/719/2125577/1?from=%2Fsearch%23sort%3Dscore%26publishedBounds%3Dfrom%26indexedBounds%3Dfrom%26tfPublications%255B0%255D%3DJe%2520suis%2520partout%26page%3D19%26searchIn%3Dall%26total%3D683&index=449.

52. "grands seigneurs absurdes, illuminés déficients, médiocres fricoteurs"

Pierre Gaxotte, "Le Personnel de la Révolution: Une Rafle à l'heure de l'apéritif," *Je Suis Partout* 447 (June 16, 1939), 1. https://www.retronews.fr/journal/je-suis-partout/16-juin-1939/719/2125553/1?from=%2Fsearch%23sort%3Dscore%26publishedBounds%3Dfrom%26indexedBounds%3Dfrom%26tfPublications

%255B0%255D%3DJe%2520suis%2520partout%26page%3D19%26searchIn%3Dall%26total%3D683&index=449.

53. Gaxotte, "Le personnel de la Revolution," 1.

54. "n'avait pas un sou"
Robert Brasillach, "Comment 'les Grands Ancêtres' ont pratiqué, bien avant nos députés, la corruption parlementaire," *Je Suis Partout* 449 (June 30, 1939): 3. https://www.retronews.fr/journal/je-suis-partout/30-juin-1939/719/2125577/1?from=%2Fsearch%23sort%3Dscore%26publishedBounds%3Dfrom%26indexed-Bounds%3Dfrom%26tfPublications%255B0%255D%3DJe%2520suis%2520partout%26page%3D19%26searchIn%3Dall%26total%3D683&index=449.

55. "Nos maîtres d'aujourd'hui, nos Danton, nos Chabot, nos Fabre d'Églantine, devraient songer qu'après nos trafics d'influence . . . nos spéculations, nos vendus, nos scandales . . . ils finiront bien par faire échouer aussi la République."
Brasillach, "Comment 'les Grands Ancêtres,'" 3.

56. "Il fallait la guerre."
P.-A. Cousteau, "La République, c'est la guerre, fraîche et joyeuse pour les lumières," *Je Suis Partout* 449 (June 30, 1939): 1. https://www.retronews.fr/journal/je-suis-partout/30-juin-1939/719/2125577/1?from=%2Fsearch%23sort%3Dscore%26publishedBounds%3Dfrom%26indexedBounds%3Dfrom%26tfPublications%255B0%255D%3DJe%2520suis%2520partout%26page%3D19%26searchIn%3Dall%26total%3D683&index=449.

57. Daniel Halévy, *Histoire d'une histoire* (Paris: Grasset, 1939), 8.

58. Halévy, *Histoire d'une histoire*, 58.

59. Halévy, *Histoire d'une histoire*, 68.

60. "ses saints et ses milices charitables."
Halévy, *Histoire d'une histoire*, 72.

61. "*Dieu, foi, priere*, ne doivent pas être prononcés devant l'enfant, ni plus par lui."
Halévy, *Histoire d'une histoire*, 72.

62. Halévy, *Histoire d'une histoire*, 10.

63. "Il faut détacher les âmes et les attacher ailleurs: les convertir."
Halévy, *Histoire d'une histoire*, 87.

64. "une idéologie dépassée, un système politique archaïque et inefficace, étayé par une classe sociale parasitaire."
Albert Soboul, *1789: An I de la Révolution* (Paris: Editions Sociales Internationales, 1939), 20.

65. "Les individus ne sont plus déterminés par la classe où ils naissent, les disinctions fondées sur la naissance étant abolies; les hommes naissent et demeurent libres et égaux en droits; il ne peut y avoir d'autre différence entre eux que celle résultant de leurs dons naturels et de l'utilité commune."
Soboul, *1789*, 335.

66. "Le peuple soulevé met fin en quelques heures à une oppression de dix siècles. Car c'est le peuple qui a tout fait. La bourgeoisie resta à l'Hôtel de Ville, économe de son sang comme de son argent, soucieuse uniquement d'éluder un conflit redoutable."

Amédée Dunois, "La liberté naissait: Ecroulement d'un monde," *Le Populaire*, no. 5992 (14 July 1939): 1. https://www.retronews.fr/journal/le-populaire-1916-1970/14-juillet-1939/110/1191355/5.

67. "La Révolution, précipitant son cours, peut préparer aux peuples anxieux les lendemains nouveaux."

Soboul, *1789*, 339.

68. "En ces années 1789–1794, au cours desquelles les frontières étaient enfoncées, les Jacobins ont pensé qu'il n'y avait pas de salut en dehors du contact avec les masses populaires. . . . *C'est pour cette raison qu'ils ont sauvé à la fois la France et la démocratie.*"

Jean Bruhat, "La Révolution Française et les masses populaires," in *Cahiers du bolchévisme: organe théorique du Parti communiste français (S.F.I.C.)*, ed. Parti communiste français, Comité central, July 1939, 991. https://gallica.bnf.fr/ark:/12148/bpt6k128314/f1.item#.

69. "Aujourd'hui se développe la théorie suivante: quand le pays est menacé, on ne donne pas la parole au peuple, on met en sommeil le parlement, on multiplie les entraves du droit de réunion."

Bruhat, "La Revolution," 991.

70. Pascal Ory, "La Commemoration révolutionnaire en 1939," in *La France et les Français en 1938–1939*, eds. René Rémond and Janine Bourdin (Paris: Presses de la Fondation nationale des sciences politiques, 1978), 130.

71. "Victorieux jusque dans leur défaite, les Français gagnèrent à leurs idées les nations mêmes qui s'étaient révoltées contre leur domination."

Edouard Herriot, *Aux Sources de la liberté* (Paris, Gallimard, 1939), 196.

72. "Il n'y a plus, cette nuit-là, de seigneurs, de prélats et de vilains. Il n'y a que des Français. La Bretagne, La Bourgogne, le Dauphiné, la Provence renoncent à leurs états. La France doit n'être désormais qu'une grande 'maison maternelle,' déclarent les députés de Lorraine. Au feu de l'enthousiasme, l'unité nationale s'accomplit."

Herriot, *Aux Sources*, 33.

73. "À l'heure où les principes démocratiques sont défiés et raillés par l'immoralisme des états dits totalitaires, ce qui nous intéresse . . . c'est d'observer qu'une telle communauté unissant la Grande Bretagne, les États-Unis et la République française crée la raison profonde et permanente de leur solidarité nécessaire et de leurs obligations envers un monde que veulent dominer les codes brutaux de la barbarie."

Herriot, *Aux Sources*, 28.

74. "Ce dynamisme de la liberté . . . sera-il épuisé?"

Herriot, *Aux Sources*, 198.

75. "Cette armée que vous acclamiez ce matin est la gardienne de vos libertés. Vous avez compris qu'elle était capable de briser toutes les attaques qui pourraient mettre en peril notre pays."

Edouard Daladier, Discours le 14 juillet 1939, *Le Figaro*, July 15, 1939. https://gallica.bnf.fr/ark:/12148/bpt6k410283j/f4.item.

76. "penser pour l'univers."

Simone Weil, *L'Enracinement*, *OC* V, Vol. 2 (Paris: Gallimard, 2013), 248.

77. "On prétend que Napoléon a propagé, les armes à la main, les idées de liberté et d'égalité de la Révolution française; mais ce qu'il a principalement propagé, c'est l'idée de l'état centralisé . . . l'état comme ainsi conçu, inventé pour ainsi dire par Richelieu, conduit à un point plus haut de la perfection par Louis XIV, à un point plus haut encore par la Révolution, puis par Napoléon, a trouvé aujourd'hui sa forme suprême en Allemagne."

Weil, "Quelques réflexions sur les origines de *l'hitlérisme*," *OC* II, Vol. 3 (Paris: Gallimard, 1989), 171.

78. "la prise de la Bastille, la nuit du 4 août, la fin des privilèges, l'avènement du peuple, et le soulèvement du peuple contre la coalition des despotes."

Jean Pierre Azéma and Michel Winock, *La IIIe République: 1870–1940*, 2nd ed. (Paris: Hachette, 1986), 174.

79. "parce que les seigneurs objectèrent que si on le réalisait les petits-fils des miliciens seraient seigneurs et leurs propres petits-fils seraient serfs."

Weil, *L'Enracinement*, 201.

80. "Il faut que [la France] apparaisse à ses propres citoyens et au monde comme une source perpétuellement jaillissante de liberté. Il ne faudrait pas que dans le monde un seul homme sincèrement amoureux de liberté pût se croire des raisons légitimes de haïr la France; il faudrait que tous les hommes sérieux qui aiment la liberté soit heureux que la France existe. Nous croyons qu'il en est ainsi, mais c'est une erreur; il dépend de nous qu'il en soit désormais ainsi."

Weil, "Réflexions en vue d'un bilan," *OC* II, Vol. 3 (Paris: Gallimard, 1989), 116.

81. "le 1917 du peuple de France."

Maurice Thorez, "Le 150e Anniversaire" (Discours à Buffalo – 26 juin 1939), in *Cahiers du bolchévisme: organe théorique du Parti communiste français (S.F.I.C.)*, ed. Parti communiste français, Comité central, July 1939, 904. https://gallica.bnf.fr/ark:/12148/bpt6k128314/f1.item#.

82. "refaire une âme au pays."

Weil, *L'Enracinement*, 233.

83. Stanley Hoffmann points to the progressive "nibbling away" at France effected by the prewar pacifist movements, those on the far left as well as those on the far right.

"The Trauma of 1940: A Disaster and Its Traces," in *The French Defeat of 1940: Reassessments*, ed. Joel Blatt (Providence: Berghahn Books, 1998), 366.

84. "la faute de negligence criminelle à l'égard de la patrie"

Simone Weil, *Cahiers*, *OC* VI, Vol. 4 (Paris: Gallimard, 2006), 375.

85. "Le désastre de la France en 1940 a posé à nouveau, sous la lumière la plus pure, la question de la Révolution française. On n'a pu obtenir la capitulation de la nation . . . qu'en agissant en premier lieu contre le patrimoine idéologique de la Grande Révolution."

Qtd. in Ory, "La Commémoration révolutionnaire en 1939," 136.

Chapter 3

The Debacle

The Debate Engaged

Germany invaded Poland on September 1, 1939. Poland's allies France and England both declared war against Germany two days afterward. In anticipation of France's entry into the war, the order for mobilization of reservists had been given on August 26. After this flurry of activity, what followed was eight months of *la drôle de guerre* (the phony war), a period of inaction marked by few military campaigns of any import besides in far-off Finland, with most French conscripts under arms waiting at their camps and caserns for the next shoe to drop.

This situation changed on May 10, 1940, when the German blitzkrieg overran France from the north and then attacked from the east through the Ardennes Forest, avoiding the highly fortified Maginot Line, the barrier touted as impregnable by French military authorities. In the wake of a series of military disasters, the government of Paul Reynaud fell and Marshall Pétain, the hero of Verdun in World War I, took the reins of government. He asked for a cease fire and negotiated the terms of an armistice, signed on June 22, 1940, which ceded the northern half of France as an "occupied" zone and retained the southern half as a "free zone," called "Vichy" after the spa town where it was centered. When the new regime gathered in Vichy after the armistice, the majority of the members of the National Assembly voted an end to the Third Republic and gave full powers to govern to Pétain on July 10. After a summit at Montoire between Hitler and Pétain on October 24, an official policy of collaboration with the German government was pursued.

France fell after a little more than a month of hostilities. This devastating collapse, termed afterward "the Debacle," placed into the German ambit the most populous (if colonies are included) and second most prosperous country (determined by GDP) in continental Western Europe; it put out of commission a military machine that had defeated Germany in 1918; it precipitated the fall of a liberal democratic Republic. In a scant two months, Republican France had lost a war to a Fascist power and had voted itself out of existence to be replaced by a one-man authoritarian regime.

These events were devastating to the French, even those who had sought a rapprochement with Fascist powers and abhorred the Republic. The announcement of the cease fire, in Henri Amouroux's terms, "relieve, but dislocate what remains that is solid (so little, in truth) in the social and military armature of France."[1] A stunned France began very quickly, however, to assess what had gone so wrong as to lead to this humiliating defeat and collapse. In the period of France's greatest uncertainty, directly after the Debacle of 1940, many engaged in an attempt to understand the causes behind the present situation: they questioned the preparation of the army and the war strategy, the ideological fault lines dividing (and weakening) the French, and the governmental system that had fallen under its own weight. But they cast their eyes not just backward but also forward to map the future. In the eyes of the greater number of French, Vichy was no more than "provisional" government, a placeholder during the time of war.[2] That France's eventual fate would depend upon the outcome of the war was clear, but that outcome was hoped for and feared rather than certain. During those months and years when the situation appeared the most uncertain (if not hopeless), some were recasting a past and imagining a future from within this flux—and very differently.

The question of how France arrived at June 1940 demanded a reconsideration of the recent and distant past. All of the various responses, no matter how far separated on the ideological or political spectrum, assumed the "official" narrative of French history—the "sacred history" promulgated by the Third Republic. As we saw in the first chapter, the Third Republic's narrative history fit within the larger master narrative of progress. France, particularly after 1789, held an outsized place in this master narrative—the French had introduced beyond their own borders and continued to champion the "progress" encompassed in the protection of "rights" and the growth and strengthening of popular representation assured by democratic institutions. They had fought to vanquish despots both domestic and foreign. How could this historical progression accommodate collapse and defeat at the hands of a Fascist power?

The fall of France, then, presented the French with a monumental challenge: the historical narrative would have to accommodate it, but how and to what degree would this event transform it? This historiographical difficulty encompassed another even more urgent question: if the history of a people offers them a mirror to themselves, what national identity would result from this transformed narrative?

The following discussion will focus on French assessments of the Debacle written *before* the final outcome of the war was clear or decided, during the time of greatest uncertainty, 1940–1943. To limit the time frame to these years selects out for certain committed voices: it takes a special kind of imagination to place bets on the table, to venture to think through the past and imagine the future in a very murky present. The discussion will treat the range of responses competing for the attention of the French people and will place Simone Weil's writings, particularly *L'Enracinement (The Need for Roots)*, within a continuum of these assessments.

Most of the works under discussion are evaluative essays or memoirs written by figures important in the intellectual landscape of the time; works created with the intent of contributing to and setting the tone for public discourse, even if not immediately published and widely known at the time; and treatments of some length, ambition, and sweep.[3] I've not focused on imaginative literature, private diaries or journals, or works of journalism. Brasillach's *Notre Avant Guerre (Our Pre-War)*, Lucien Rebatet's *Les Décombres (Rubble)*, both bestsellers of the occupation years, Marc Bloch's *L'Étrange Défaite (The Strange Defeat)*, Léon Blum's *À l'Échelle humaine (On a Human Scale)* (two of the works most referred to in histories of the occupation years), the foundational speeches of Philippe Pétain and Charles De Gaulle, these and other texts will allow me to posit a "horizon of expectations" (to borrow a term from Hans Robert Jauss's reception theory) within which to place Simone Weil's own writings of the period.[4]

In truth, though the defeat demanded adjustments to the official historical narrative, some of these reassessments were being prepared before the event itself, as we saw in the preceding chapter. Weil and others had already been reworking and reevaluating the French historical narrative before June of 1940 and were thus ready with an analysis that the defeat itself merely confirmed, in their eyes.

Several concerns recur in these different early assessments of the defeat. One is a focus on its enormity and thus historical significance. Certain writers see it as cataclysmic, with deep causes, traceable to ideological, moral, and even spiritual failings on the part of the French. Concomitantly, such a cataclysmic event calls for the dismantling of official French history and the creation or reassertion of another one. Many of these writers are on the right, but not all. I would place Weil in this category of response. Other writers, while admitting the enormity of the defeat, limit its causes and thus its import. They focus, for example, on the military nature of the defeat, or on the failings of a narrow stratum of the population. Thus contained, the defeat does not demand a fundamental recasting of the official narrative, can, in fact, reaffirm it.

One did not have to be an imbecile or hopeless pessimist to foresee German victory on all fronts in 1940. Both "common sense" and "realism" could have easily led to that conclusion. Indeed, it required a certain stubborn hope and courage to imagine another outcome. And Vichy and other collaborationist groups would have no truck with impractical hope; they preached the necessity of facing hard realities.

These "realists" exhorted their compatriots to take a commonsense stance toward the defeat: to drop a "pointless sulking,"[5] to admit their own and England's defeat, to accept a probable long-term German domination of Europe, and to come to some kind of accommodation with the victor. Jean Weiland, the vice-president of the group *Collaboration franco-allemande* (French-German Collaboration), made the following statement in December 1940 in one of a series of talks in Paris:

> All the propagandas of the world will not prevail against this evidence: England lost the war, as we did . . .
>
> Even if it stands up to the bombings for a longer or lesser amount of time, even if it tries to move the battlefield to Africa or elsewhere, that changes nothing in the situation in Europe. Europe will remake itself without England.[6]

The Fascist anti-Semite Lucien Rebatet expressed a similar view, comparing the gains of totalitarian states versus those of democracies in the recent past:

> On one side, two hundred fifty million inhabitants, of which 20 million are soldiers, living on the richest and most civilized lands of the Old World. On the other side, thirty-three million beings, half of them savages, in territories that are three-fourths desert guarded by fifty or sixty thousand soldiers.
>
> The good liberal peoples of the West nonetheless still anticipate the immanent triumph of the democracies with a smiling confidence
>
> Let's leave those sweet idiots aside for an instant.[7]

How very inadequate and short-sighted what passed for hard-bitten realism *then* appears *now*.

These writers insist upon the fact that the Debacle was not merely a military defeat, where the number of French combatants and amount and quality of French war materiel were outmatched by the opponent. It resulted instead from a moral and even spiritual collapse. This interpretation resounded from church pulpits as well as official governmental addresses in the months following the defeat. Marshall Pétain set a tone of national self-castigation in his first address to the French people, identifying "the moral bankruptcy of the pre-war years."[8] The call for a moral and spiritual self-critique was taken up by many other figures during this period, not all, of course, collaborationists or Vichy sympathizers, but none did it serve better than these. The French are called to expiate those sins and errors of "the pre-war years," a shorthand for the government, the ideology and public figures of the Third Republic as a whole. The French people had been seduced and the nation ruined by a gamut of Republican figures: those who allowed "the spirit of pleasure" to prevail over "the spirit of sacrifice," who preferred to make demands rather than to serve, in Pétain's phrases;[9] "cretinous civil servants, harmful politicians, thick-headed teachers, unions, agents of the lodges and the ghettoes, corrupt financiers,"[10] in Weiland's terms; "France—Jewish and democratic, vulgarized, brainwashed, ludicrous,"[11] in Rebatet's characteristically more rabid style—in short, the usual suspects of the right and extreme right.

The absoluteness of the defeat deprives the French Republic and its version of historical progress of any credibility and validity, in their view. It argues for a complete break with that past and with French "sacred history."

> The first order of business for us was to absolutely liquidate our past. . . . As for the institutions of the regime, to which we didn't even have to bother to deliver the coup de grace, the Panzer divisions had flung everything to the ground. All we had to do was push the pieces into the offal pile.[12]

Rebatat invites his countrymen and -woman to a national purging of the past, a purifying ceremony in which all traces of sympathy with the French Republic can be eliminated.

On the other side of the spectrum are those who contain or minimize the significance and long-term impact of the Debacle. This event, so minimized, can still be included in the existing historical narrative and does not necessitate huge adjustment to it.

Léon Blum, head of the Socialist Party and former prime minister of the Popular Front government, offers a powerful riposte to the arguments outlined above both in his memoir *A l'Echelle humaine (On a Human Scale)* and in his testimony during the Riom Trial, which will be discussed later in this chapter. His memoir, written in prison and smuggled out while he was awaiting trial, was shared clandestinely before it was published in 1945. In both his memoir and his trial testimony, he insists on the importance of understanding how the defeat occurred, but he wants to disentangle cause from fault, error from sin, responsibility from guilt, wants his compatriots to see the defeat as a secular rather than millenarian event. He saw clearly that the Vichy party line of "an almost perverse mania for self-flagellation"[13] was being used as a way to discredit recent French history, in particular the Third Republic government, liberal democratic principles, and the entire legacy of the Revolution.

While admitting that the immediate impact of the defeat was a numbing blow, Blum quickly turns to containing its import by several strategies. He first insists upon the defeat as a "mere" military event, not God's or history's referendum on France's virtues and vices. He puts the Debacle into a continuum of other recent defeats from which France was quickly able to recover—Waterloo (during the Napoleonic Wars) and Sedan and Metz (during the Franco-Prussian War).[14] He also places June 1940 in the context of a broader world history over several millennia—Greek and Israelite defeats that led the people to question what they had done to call down on themselves the punishment of the gods, a natural but primitive impulse.[15] This effort to find analogous events that evoke analogous reactions takes the defeat out of the category of the singular and incomparable. The repeatable and recognizable lacks the numinous aura of a unique event, is somehow minimized.

Marc Bloch, a founding member of the Annales School of historical study and a combatant in 1940, wrote his assessment of the campaign, *L'Étrange Défaite* (*The Strange Defeat*), directly after the military rout. It existed in manuscript form and, like Blum's memoirs, was published only after the end of the war in 1946 by a Resistance press, *Le Franc Tireur* (Sniper). Bloch, unlike Blum, did not survive the war; he joined the Resistance, was captured, imprisoned, tortured (he was personally interrogated by Klaus Barbie, the "butcher of Lyon"), and shot by the Gestapo in 1944.

Like Blum, Bloch attempts to contain the import of the defeat by insisting upon its military causes and, further, tracing these back to one specific group—the high command and the professional officer corps. Fully a third of the book consists of a series of examples and telling anecdotes to support his claim of the "incapacity of the high command,"[16] incidents which he either witnessed first-hand as an active officer during the campaign or those he learned of from others but whose credibility he is willing to vouchsafe. Tale follows tale of blunders by high officers, of their incompetence, of the insufficiencies of intelligence services, the lack of communication between different armies and different services—in short, an unforgiving indictment of that body whose task it was to ensure the integrity and survival of the French nation.

Although Bloch cites specific blunders on the part of individual officers that, in their aggregate, certainly contributed to the Debacle, what is most important for him is the failure of the officer corps' "intellectual training," inculcated in the *École de Guerre* (War College) and incubated during the decades separating World Wars I and II. He anticipates later historians in studying the Debacle as the result of the lessons of history gone awry. "Our leaders, in the midst of many contradictions, claimed, above all, to repeat, in 1940, the war of 1915–1918. The Germans waged a 1940 war."[17] Henri Amouroux seconds this assertion:

> Facing a German army free of all of its references, modern in its technique as well as in its strategic thinking, our newspapers, our generals, our ministers to the bitter end cling to the memories of 1914–1918, is if it were possible to plagiarize courage, success, glory.[18]

Rather than a war fought in stable lines where distances and victories were measured in meters, the campaign of 1940 was characterized by the speed of the German advance and the kilometers it was able to devour.[19] The front was a constantly shifting and uncertain construct rather than a tangible line. German initiative and improvisation met with French implementation of strategies drawn up long beforehand and little suited for an ever-moving line of battle.[20] Finally, those arms and strategies that had won the war in 1918 were trotted out again in 1940, while the innovations developed in the meantime—motorized units, tanks used as an offensive weapon, and bombardment by air[21]—were viewed with suspicion.

These military blunders, this short-sightedness on the part of the high command, are what Bloch terms the "direct cause" of the war. In the following section, he contemplates its "deep causes," considering in turn all those various scapegoats being offered up at the time. "We have just suffered an unbelievable defeat. Who is to blame? The parliamentary system, the troops, the English, the fifth column, answer our generals. Everyone, in short, except them."[22] He disentangles each "culprit" and entertains it seriously. Were the trade unions at fault, which during a time of national crisis were more attentive to assuring their "daily bread" and keeping their own work production to a comfortable level than going into overdrive to produce materiel important to national defense? Were the pacifist and internationalist movements implicated, which heeded the call to recognize their brotherhood with the German working classes and so resisted the call to fight them? How do they feel now, Bloch asks, reduced to hunger and at the mercy of the occupier? Was the parliamentary system, riddled by intrigue, to blame? Bloch stops short at identifying these as the "profound causes" of the war. Rather, he brings the focus back once again to the failure of the officer corps. These other factors contributed, but primarily because they were seen to do so by the class that produced the officer corps—the bourgeoisie. They can only be termed the "profound causes" of the Debacle because their wholesale adoption by members of the officer corps undermined that body's loyalty to the government and very nation whose integrity and safety they had undertaken to protect.

> They only accepted the disaster with rage in their hearts. They accepted it, though, too early, because they found in it these atrocious consolations: to crush, under France's ruins, a reviled system: to bend their knees before the punishment that destiny had sent to a guilty nation.[23]

Bloch's treatment of the direct and deep causes of the war does nothing to loosen the structure of the official French historical narrative; it functions instead firmly within it and indeed affirms it. His discussion assumes the existence of class conflicts and their stubborn persistence; the right poses the main danger to France and her Republic in that group's resistance to change and progress (here in military and historical terms). The onus of the defeat lies on the shoulders of a narrow group that both blundered and, after, worked to undermine the Republic, who took a national crisis and turned it into a national calamity.

He brings his authority as an historian to bear on identifying the main fault of the war strategy. The changes that had occurred in many different arenas—ideological, technical, and social—had not been registered by the military high command. "The historian ... knows well that two wars that follow upon each other, if, in the meantime, the social structure, techniques, mindset have transformed, will never be the same war."[24]

And recent history, for the person who has eyes to see, could have served as a predictor for how this small cadre and the class that produced it would act in this particular war.

> In truth, that the parties qualified as "on the right" are so quick today to bow before the defeat, an historian can't feel a keen surprise about it. Such has been their constant tradition almost the whole of our destiny, from the Restauration to the Assembly at Versailles [when the Third Republic was being formed in 1871].[25]

This group, according to Bloch, has never recognized nor resonated to what he terms France's "deep source,"[26] its "authentic patrimony"[27]—the history of the French *collectivé* and its progress, virtue as the mainspring to the state. Bloch follows the development of this collective, and he identifies those defining moments at which it came to greater self-awareness. Those who do not recognize the beauty of these same moments set themselves outside of the French historical narrative, naysayers and jeerers rather than partakers.

> There are two categories of French who will never understand the history of France, those who refuse to resonate to the memory of the coronation at Reims [of Charles VII thanks to the efforts of Joan of Arc]; those who read with no emotion the account of the Celebration of Federation [July 14th, 1790, when representatives from all over France went to Paris to commemorate the Revolution and pledge allegiance to the new Constitution]. It little matters the present orientation of their preferences. Their impermeability to the most beautiful outpouring of collective enthusiasm is enough to condemn them.[28]

And despite his unwillingness to defend the governments of the Popular Front, quite clearly the *élan* that provided its energy and support belongs squarely within the narrative of "authentic" French history, a history that stands diametrically opposed to that espoused by the "self-styled apostles of tradition,"[29] the supporters of Vichy's *Révolution nationale*. If they, too, turn to the past to support their cause, it is a nostalgic past of a return to the soil, a nation made up of agricultural collectives rather than the ever more self-aware political *collectivités* Bloch identifies. Vichy offers up a view of French history that feeds only too well into the Nazi plans for a vassal Europe—the wish fulfillment of the victor and a nightmare for the vanquished, in Bloch's view.[30]

While characterizing the defeat as the "the most dreadful collapse"[31] of French history, in no way minimizing its horror, Bloch's treatment of the "direct causes" maintains a narrow focus on a professional cadre, while his "profound causes" keeps our attention on the malaise of that cadre and the class which produced it. The spirit of the nation is never called into question. In fact, Bloch exempts a good number of his fellow officers from his critique, and whenever he writes of the *poilu* or enlisted man, it is with recognition of his good will and courage. Part of the nation rather than the whole nation is to blame for this defeat. The ideals, the direction, the official history still hold good, need not be brought into question. Those most responsible for the defeat have deliberately removed themselves from this history, thwarted its progress whenever it could, and trumped up an "alternate" history to substitute for it. Bloch's biographer Carol Fink succinctly states all the failures he identified in the 1940 campaign: "France's defeat was the result of a gigantic false perception: the misreading of its people, the enemy, and history itself."[32]

The Riom Trials, held from February to May 1942 in the town of that name, were intended as a show trial for the collaborationist government of Pétain. It was to be no less than a national purge of the Third Republic from the French body politic by singling out certain figures closely identified with it, bringing them before the tribunal, condemning them and, metonymically, the Republic they served. Thus did Vichy hope to distance itself from a certain tradition of French historical development, write it off as both an evolutionary dead end and aberration, and relegate it to the trash bin of history. Historians have remarked how much in their interest it was for supporters of Vichy and collaboration to present the defeat as an event that marked a total break with the past[33]—they could claim a vacuum of legitimate ideas and leadership that demanded their intervention and innovations. The trial went wonderfully wrong for the Vichy government from its outset, and one of the main reasons is the brilliance and eloquence of the defendants, particularly Léon Blum and Édouard Daladier, the head of government right up to the outbreak of hostilities.

The trial unwittingly gave the eloquent Blum a megaphone, for his testimony was closely covered and widely disseminated in the press. The Riom Trials brought Blum and four other high officials of the Third Republic forward on charges of "unpreparedness for war in France from 1936–1940"[34] and "for having failed in the duties they were charged with during the critical period when they were in power."[35] While Blum addresses the particular indictments directly and systematically, he never loses from sight the clear subtext of the charges, evidenced by the prosecutor's decision to backdate their charges to the significant year 1936—French Republicanism, as it reached its apogee under the Popular Front government, is on trial, as is the vision of French history and development that it champions, and it is these that he is determined to defend.

Blum sees clearly that the trial, in locating the blame for the defeat within Popular Front policy (workers' strikes and takeovers of factories, the 40-hour work week and paid vacations that slowed down production of war materiel), was an attempt to back-build from military defeat to suggest the dangerous aberration that was the French Republic. He defends the Third Republic against the attack from the right—as against the corruption of that government, he counters with the probity of most of its politicians and institutions; as against the "easy pleasure-seeking" of the French worker, he posits the productivity and work ethic of the working class in those years.

He knew the most important battle in the trial was that over which version of French history would prevail, the Republican or anti-Republican. His final prepared statement at his trial highlights this.

> Gentlemen, I have finished. Naturally, you can find us guilty. I believe, even by your judgement, you can't erase our work. I believe you will not be able to—the word will perhaps appear haughty to you—banish us from the history of this country. We mean no presumptuousness, but we carry a certain pride: in a very perilous time we personified and invigorated the authentic tradition of our country, which is the democratic and republican tradition. Within this tradition, over history, we will, in spite of everything, have represented a moment. We are not some kind of monstrous excrescence in the history of this country because we were a popular government; we are within the tradition of this country since the French Revolution. We did not disrupt the chain, we didn't break it, we reconnected it and secured it.[36]

In this close to his testimony, he reasserts the validity of the Third Republic "sacred narrative" and the larger master narrative of progress. Indeed, so strongly does he hold to the narrative of progress that he ponders if, in the future, it might not be robust enough to coopt the terrible events of the war to itself.

> Who knows? A century or two from now, when thinkers will consider in perfect serenity the unfolding of our age, perhaps they will go so far as to conclude

that Nazism and fascism themselves played a role in this providential march of progress.[37]

The speeches and *"appels"* (appeals) of Charles De Gaulle, the leader of the Free French Forces, resonate in important ways with Blum's and Bloch's analyses without sharing their implicit support of the French Third Republic. He, too, focuses upon the defeat as a military matter, a "technical aberration," as were other defeats from which France was able to rise again, Crécy (which the French lost to the English in 1346 during the Hundred Years' War) and Sedan (which Napoleon III lost to the Prussians in 1870 during the Franco-Prussian War).[38] And De Gaulle is clear on who should take the greatest blame for it—not an entire nation, but a small cadre of policy makers, and, in particular, the military figure who is now blaming the defeat on the "guilt" (*culpabilité*) of all the French—Pétain.

> You, who presided over our military organization after the war 1914–1918, you who were Generalissimo until 1932. . . . You who were the Minister of War in 1938, you who were the highest military figure of our country, did you ever support, ask for, demand the reform that was indispensable for this system?[39]

He, too, warns against the calls to collective expiation, explaining how well such a strategy serves those who should really bear the guilt, how welcome it also is to the occupying power.

> This excess of grief and this abandon would play into our enemies' hands.
> The slogan of a sinful France, justly punished for her faults, who rushes to expiation, this is what suits completely our victors of the day. This is what responds all too well to the remorse and the self-interest of those who capitulated.[40]

While Blum and Bloch, significantly, confine their historical references largely to post-Revolutionary events and figures, in such a way as to evoke as living and adequate and robust Republican sacred history, De Gaulle makes wider gestures to a longer tradition of historical events and figures, within which the Republic plays a major but not perhaps defining role. And while Blum and Bloch are engaged in a defense of Republican sacred history, De Gaulle uses French history as a strategic weapon—he evokes it in such a way as to demonstrate that Vichy is the aberration within it. And, appropriately, the history he evokes early on is military. "London July 2, 1940: Joan of Arc, Richelieu, Louis XIV, Carnot, Napoleon, Gambetta, Poincaré, Clemenceau, Marshall Foch, would they have ever agreed to surrender France's arms to her enemies to be used against the Allies?"[41] The French tradition he recalls directly after the defeat is composed of military and political figures active during France's greatest crises, from the Hundred Years' War (Joan of Arc) to the Franco-Prussian War (Gambetta) to the Boulanger threat (Carnot) to World War I (Poincaré, Clemenceau, and Marshall Foch). None had ever consented to cede so much to the enemy, even when holding the losing hand, as Gambetta did during the siege of Paris. These heroic figures show up the Vichy government and its figures as craven.

De Gaulle calls upon the 1789 Revolution as well, again as a way of evoking a backdrop against which the *Révolution nationale*, the reimagining of France proposed by the Vichy government, can be viewed and judged. If France is to be reborn and renewed, as it was during that earlier Revolution, it needs new actors and new ideas (De Gaulle and his circle, naturally), not figures from previous regimes who have been trotted out and dusted off for this work. The "usual suspects" would be able to produce no more than a faded simulacrum of what has already existed.

> People are surprised not to find among our number worn out politicians, somnolent academicians, businessmen maneuvered by deals, washed up ranking generals, and remind us of those backward creatures of the little courts of Europe who, during the last French Revolution, took offense at not seeing Turgot, Necker and Laménie de Brienne serving on the Committee of Public Safety. What do you want? A France in revolution always prefers to win the war with General Hoche than lose it with Marshall de Soubise. To proclaim and impose the Declaration of Rights, a France in revolution always prefers to listen to Danton than to fall asleep to the drone of outdated formulas.[42]

De Gaulle's is a broader, more inclusive history than that emphasized in French Republican history. This historical record shows a mixture of errors and failures, but these amount to nothing in the face of "the enormous sum of France's merits and virtues."[43] Despite this mixed and ambiguous balance sheet, France has always been and is in 1940 basically sound. The government that capitulated without having continued an honorable fight, that in a fell swoop destroyed France's institutions and all popular representation, that accepted both servitude and collaboration with the enemy, cannot have held in mind the continuity of French tradition through all the good and bad events De Gaulle evokes. They were lacking this historic sense and, indeed, put themselves completely outside of the French historic continuum.[44] It is they who are an aberration in French history, a "monstrous excrescence," to use Blum's words.

If the historical narrative does not call for revision, the future that would follow from it and continue it does not, either. Bloch is hopeful about this future and addresses his analysis to those who will shape it. While trusting they will do much that is new, he does not want them to stray from their "authentic patrimony," that of popular collectivities and the mainspring of virtue. The true France, the authentic France, as opposed to that packaged by the right and pleasing to the victor, is the France of the *philosophes* and the Revolution, that France that is a byword for civilization.

Blum's imagined future, too, does not stray too far from the Republican past. It will include, he trusts, the reestablishment of the parliamentary system, the persistence of social democratic principles, and internationalism in the form of a rebirth of a League of Nations. As it indeed did.

De Gaulle has good reasons to be cagier about his vision of the future, especially its political cast, so does not offer as clear an outline for it as do Bloch and Blum. It will, of course, honor the "liberties" of which Vichy had deprived the French, will probably take the form of a legislative assembly with links to that "earlier" one (*d'autrefois*),[45] but no much more concrete vision is offered. The main goal was to win the war and drive the Germans from France, and political infighting among the Free French over details of the postwar could not be allowed to derail that process.[46]

For all their ideological differences, in delimiting the import of the defeat, in incorporating it into a continuum of French historical development, all three are engaged in an ideological contest to safeguard a certain form of the French historical narrative against an opponent who is attempting to dismantle it and is using the Debacle itself as the launching site for this attack.[47]

Once the right and far right have summarily relegated the Third Republic and its sacred history to the trash bin of history, what "authentic France" do they evoke, to what historical narrative can they connect to derive legitimacy and resonance? This alternative history might be summed up by Vichy's *Révolution nationale*, its ambitious plans for "rebuilding" France. The policies it had laid out involved proposals to create administrative units in France that adhered more closely to historical provinces in an effort to return to regional identities and affiliations (regionalism); to renew agrarian life in France by enticing urban populations back to the countryside to work the land with promises of land grants and support in terms of technical expertise (agrarianism); to bring the Church back from the Siberian wilds it had been exiled to during the Republic to make it a center of communal life; to refocus French education to emphasize more on trades and agriculture;[48] to reorganize schools to peddle back the strict secularism imposed by the Third Republic and to focus curricula more upon the beneficial role of the Church and the monarchy in French history, both excised from Republican classrooms[49]—a Revolution that can be characterized as "back to the future." Many of these initiatives ended stillborn—given Vichy's precarious hold on long-term power, there was little incentive to bring them to successful completion.[50] In addition, several that had been initiated met with insurmountable challenges:

the shortage of paper made the production of new school texts impossible, and there were relatively few willing to take on the rigors of going from the city "back" to the land.[51]

The educational reforms proposed by Vichy offer some indication of its version of French history. A shared tenet of these reforms was the view that the Revolution held an inordinate role in Republican sacred history and thus in the textbooks of the Republic. That event, it was believed, was highlighted in a way that deformed "real" French history. An article in a Catholic newspaper stated this position:

> One could have believed that France hadn't begun to know glory, prosperity except after the Revolution, and that before there was nothing but poverty, darkness and wars. One thus erased fifteen centuries of history, centuries such as the 13th or the 17th, when France enjoyed incomparable prosperity and prestige in the world.[52]

Vichy's version of French history would give more emphasis to pre-1789 history, those centuries and figures who had contributed to France's greatness, conceived in terms of glory, prosperity, and prestige. This version highlighted a march of progress, but central to these were forces and institutions excluded from the Enlightener's narrative—the Church and the monarchy as civilizing forces.[53] There was an effort to "desacralize" the Revolution by insisting upon its more mundane causes—the preceding financial crises and bad harvests, for example. In this view, its final legacy was a negative one—it left a nation very divided along class and ideological lines, an argument we saw in the preceding chapter in Daniel Halévy's *History of a History*.[54]

But it proved difficult to supplant the Republican historical narrative, to impose an alternate pattern on French history's events. This difficulty had made itself felt before the war as well, for example during the celebrations and reevaluations surrounding the 150th anniversary of the French Revolution in 1939, as we saw previously. Although the tensions between different political groups and the implicit agendas to which they wished to bend this celebration made it a challenge to turn it into a celebration of French "unity," the groups on the right made perhaps the least compelling use of it. They of course focused their polemic on the Terror, the September massacres, the Revolutionary tribunal in an attempt to discredit the entire Revolution on the basis of these moments of excess, but this ploy proved merely a destructive one. They attempted to pull down the prevailing narrative but had difficulty offering an alternative one.

Against the *grands ancêtres*, those commanding even if controversial figures such as Robespierre, Danton, the Abbe Sièyes, who is showcased by the far right? The editors of *Je Suis Partout* dedicate their commemorative issue on the Revolution thus:

> This issue is dedicated to those who fought, by all [possible] means, against revolutionary barbarity, and, particularly, to the PEASANTS OF THE VENDEE who died for the truth, as well as to the high and holy memory of Charlotte de Corday.[55]

The Vendéens waged a royalist revolt against the Revolution from 1793 to 1795 in the west of France, and Charlotte Corday famously murdered the Montagnard Revolutionary leader Marat in his bath. In his 1938 *Les Lys sanglants: roman historique (The Bleeding Lilies: An Historic Novel)*, Léon Daudet wrote an encomium to Marie Antoinette in an effort to transform her into a hero of the Counter-Revolution.[56] None of these counter figures have the heft and resonance needed to combat the *grands ancêtres* of the Republican narrative. Pascal Ory outlines the difficulties faced by anti-Republicans in their smear campaign against the Revolution.

> However violent it might have been, the refusal on the part of the counter-revolutionaries remains within the limits of verb. In order for it to turn into a response, it would have been necessary for Louis XIV, Racine or Olivier de Serres, without mentioning Grégoire de Tours, celebrated within the most conservative circles, to measure up in memory to '89.[57]

The figures singled out by the right include the autocratic sun king, the brilliant playwright with Jansenist leanings who served later in life in the court of Louis XIV, the author of a compendium of the best agricultural practices available in 1600, and the sixth-century bishop of Tours who wrote histories of the Merovingians and hagiographies intended to combat heresies—a mixed bag of heroes to put up against Danton, Mirabeau, and Robespierre.

Even when the right does evoke certain events that could stand as foundational for their version of French history, they are unable to connect these into a narrative that gives them élan and meaning, and they prove incapable of singling out figures who might give them imaginative resonance. These events are recounted as isolated miscarriages. The attempted coup d'état of February 6, 1934, recurs in the writings of right-wing writers but fails in these treatments to achieve the status of a numinous event. As recounted by both Brasillach and Rebatet, faceless crowds gather, react, and are dispersed. No individual face or figure emerges from the crowd to compel enthusiasm. Rebatet, in bemoaning the fact that the army had never heeded the call to overturn the Republic, recounts a series of discrete failures and abortive attempts to make history.

> Leon Daudet, in his charming *Souvenirs (Memories)*, asserts with affability that, at each crisis of the Republic, a general, even a colonel intent on energetic action would have sufficed for the regime to pass from life to death. It is at least plausible, if you think about that unfortunate imbecile Boulanger, who didn't have 500 meters to go from the Madeleine to the Elysée [palace of the French president] to become the master of France, and who didn't dare cover them.[58]

In this lament, Rebatet unwittingly tells a more significant tale about his own cause. He and others on the far right find it difficult to posit an alternative history that can compete with and supplant French Republican history. Theirs are singularly unmoving constructs, barren of sacred dates or "narrative events," without a stirring "initial situation," poor in compelling "heroes," in short any of those elements necessary to galvanize the attention and imagination of those who would seek their national identity within it. Indeed, it would be almost impossible to imagine the French being able to devote any love or loyalty to it. These writers are singularly incapable of calling upon a "collective memory"—an event that will have the following function: "to reactivate, 'in the eyes of all' . . . one of the elements of its legitimacy, most often a founding event or figure, the objective being to constitute a retrospective consensus."[59] They can tear down and declare defunct Republican sacred history but cannot construct a viable alternate to it.

Weil, who in 1933 had written, "And I search in vain for any reason whatsoever why I should cherish with less fraternal feelings my German comrades, known and unknown, than any random French people,"[60] offers in 1943 this searing metaphor for loss and exile: "[The French] know that a part of their soul is so attached to France that when France is removed, the soul remains attached to it, like the skin on a burning object, and so is ripped off."[61]

In summer and early fall of 1942 Weil found herself in New York City, having accompanied her parents there into exile. Her physical distance from France and her own relative ease and safety in comparison to her countrymen and -women were intolerable to her. From the moment of her arrival, she made concerted efforts to return to Europe to take part in the Free French efforts centered in London and hoped eventually to be sent to France for clandestine operations. She sent numerous letters to schoolmates well situated within the London circles and made her case in person when they passed through New York. Her *École Normale Supérieure* classmate Maurice Schumann, De Gaulle's spokesman, was able to secure her an invitation to join the Free France organization in London, where she arrived in October of 1942.

She joined a working group of the *Comité Général d'Etudes* (CGE) (General Committee for Studies), the Free French "Brain Trust" charged with planning for a post-occupation France. Different groups were preparing position papers on a range of problems that France would face postwar: how to conduct the trials of collaborators and abrogate the laws passed by Vichy; the form of constitution best suited to avoid the pitfalls of that of the Third Republic; whether to allow a range of political parties or establish a one-party system; and the future status of French colonies.[62] These papers were circulated, and some landed on Weil's desk for her comment. She wrote several short responses to various proposals specifically for the committee—on the bases for legitimacy of the provisional government, on plans for a new constitution, on the role of political parties, for example—and others on topics about which her views were not solicited—the future of the French colonies.

Policies and governmental structures were being proposed by the different working groups, and as Weil came to understand the priorities of the CGE and *la France combattante*, she developed serious reservations about them. It was premature, in her view, to entertain proposals for policy or forms of government. Any planning for the future should be preceded by considerations of the principles—"*les notions fondamentales*"[63]—that could serve as the basis for reimagining and rebuilding France. To propose structures and policies beforehand was to put the cart before the horses.[64]

In London, then, Weil's work follows two tracks: she responds to specific proposals about France's future as a member of the CGE. More importantly, she lays out the "fundamental notions" that should serve as the basis for that future in a work written in the last months of her life and published posthumously under the title *L'Enracinement* or *The Need for Roots*.

Weil begins this essay by laying out the most fundamental of questions in the section titled "*Prélude à une déclaration des devoirs envers l'être humain*" ("Prelude to a declaration of obligations toward the human being"):[65] What are the needs of the human soul? To what degree can a political system be set up to permit these needs to be met?[66] This "declaration" resonates with other similar ones that lay down the principles behind governance, in particular the 1789 Declaration of the Rights of Man and of the Citizen, drawn up by France's Revolutionary Constituent Assembly.

The Declaration of 1789 focuses on rights and the limits (*bornes*) established to protect those rights, to prevent governments and other individuals from impinging on them. Weil believed this focus on rights and limits was misbegotten. She emphasizes in her declaration the obligations owed to a human being. Interestingly, there was a heated discussion during the drafting of the 1789 Declaration about whether to include obligations as a corollary to rights in the document: the Abbé Grégoire and other representatives of the clergy argued that rights must necessarily be accompanied by duties that paralleled and restricted them,[67] and one representative emphasized the importance of counterweighing the "egoism and pride" entailed in a focus on rights by the "corrective" of duties.[68] The majority of the Revolutionary Assembly voted against including duties, so they were not added; in Weil's declaration they serve as the center of gravity. *The Need for Roots* recognizes many of the rights safeguarded in the French Declaration of 1789—liberty, equality, property, and free speech—but adds others—order, hierarchy, honor, risk, and truth— and the final need that will inform the rest of her work—*The Need for Roots*.

Even the naming of these needs is a challenge to what is being discussed in Resistance circles.

> There is a terrible responsibility. Because it entails what can be called remaking the soul of a country; and there is such a strong temptation to remake it with strokes of lies or partial truths that something more than heroism is needed to attach oneself to truth.[69]

To address *the needs of the soul* ups the ante for those who are planning for France's future.

Weil understands that defeat and occupation had even further corroded a French soul already hallowed out by years of untruths and half-truths, those conveyed in its sacred history. She fears for her country after the occupation; during the war years the French were learning to despise and disregard their government and the forces of order, both the Germans and Vichy. They were on the precipice of being a lawless nation. But this lack of feeling for their country was evident even before the war began—if France foundered in 1940, it was because they had loved it so little that they had let it "drop from their hands."[70]

France's soul can be "remade" through loving attention given to a worthy object, and for the French that worthy object could and should be France itself.

> To give the French something to love. And to give them first of all France to love. To conceive the reality corresponding to the name of France in such a way that, just as she is, in her truth, she can be loved with the entire soul.[71]

But this refashioned soul must be able to contemplate France with no veils of lies and half-truths obscuring "her truth." And the only pathway to knowing France "just as she is" is through her past. Weil writes that "we possess no other life, no other sap but the treasures inherited from the past and digested, assimilated, recreated by us. Of all of the needs of the human soul, there is none more vital than the past."[72] In 1940, however, the French had "vomited" their past.[73]

Here, then, is another of Weil's "fundamental notions": a shared past provides an image of France that her people can love, and at that point in time, it was imperative that they love something with all their hearts. And through an understanding of this past the collective soul is forged. These operating assumptions serve to orient her critique of contemporary discussions of France's history, and her first task is to prove how poorly extant versions of official French history have served these ends.

Weil is firmly in the camp of those who believe the Debacle cannot and should not be contained within the category of a mere "military defeat"—it was a catastrophe that showed up the insufficiencies of the government and the French identity formed by the historical narrative. It represented both a moral and spiritual collapse for France. All of its members were disaffected and crumbled before the German onslaught, the proletariat reduced to "a state of apathetic stupor," the bourgeoisie "gnawed" at by their money, and the peasantry demoralized by having served as "cannon fodder" in the Great War.[74] And in Weil's view the "official line" of French history, the Third Republic's keywords of "Liberté, Egalité et Fraternité," constituted the lies that had empoisoned French society and made it ripe for its fall: the Republic had gotten ahead of itself by reaching for lofty concepts beyond its capacity to realize them.[75] The catastrophe was largely traceable to the defects of the government and its concept of nation, and it marked the death of both. There is no need to attempt to model the future on this "sacred" past, to argue any continuity from it, since it has no legitimacy.

And Weil will not quibble about the details of the versions of French history proffered by Republicans and anti-Republicans. Despite some small discrepancies between these two narratives, they both tell the same story, in her view. Both versions enshrine progress in the form of an historical movement toward centralization, uniformity of custom and culture, expansion, and annexation. Both invite the French people to love their country because of its grandeur and power, valorize prestige and force. These are the underlying, operative values that they offer to the French to love; this is the mirror they hold up to them.

Nothing could be more mistaken, in her view, than to brace up failing French spirits with such celebrations of France's glorious past. France's present situation called for the pity and compassion of her citizens, not pride.

> To evoke at this moment the historical grandeur of France, her past and future glories, the brilliance by which her existence has been surrounded, that's not possible without a kind of inner rigidity that gives something forced to the tone. Nothing which resembles pride is appropriate for those who are wretched.[76]

This comment serves as a strong rejoinder to the evocations of France's glorious past made by De Gaulle and others.

But Weil does not leave her critique of these two different versions of the French historical narrative at that. If the right's attack on that narrative and effort to replace it with another had proved anything, it had proved how robust that official narrative was, how virtually impossible to dislodge. For the most part, thinkers on the right had come up with a shadow, parallel narrative, but one focusing on losing battles and non-starter figures. This constituted no more than a negative image, reactive history, still parasitically dependent for existence upon the official one. Weil knew it would take more drastic measures, a more radical strategy to displace that narrative. The first step in this process is to show that the French historical narrative could not only accommodate the Debacle but indeed could claim it as its logical endpoint and the apotheosis of the "progress" which was its motor.

Official French history has enshrined the "civilizing" Roman heritage, the conquest of new territories under the monarchs, the centralization and homogenization effected by Richelieu and Louis XIV, and the Revolution's work to meld a group of "conquered territories" into a "nation," as we saw in the first chapter. Progress is premised upon the development of larger political units, fewer local, regional identifications in favor of more catholic ones, and power increasingly centralized and placed in the hands of a larger state machine, this all accomplished through the use of force. And the world had seen the logical closure to such a history. Hitler's rise is not a "German" problem at all, but the apotheosis of this trajectory. Weil imagines someone asking, in 1939,

> For progress, for the fulfillment of History, perhaps it's necessary to go that way . . . France had the victory in 1918; she wasn't able to accomplish the unity of Europe; now Germany is trying to accomplish it; let's not stand in the way.[77]

In so presenting Hitler within this narrative of progress as the figure who was able to create a "united" Europe out of smaller political and cultural entities, Weil treats Hitler's brutal annexation not as an historical fluke but as a logical result of the course taken by Western development. In identifying Hitler as the endpoint to an historical progression, Weil fundamentally discredits the French official history and its sacred events. Single plot elements—annexation, growth of larger political entities through absorbing smaller ones, and military campaigns—are taken out of the familiar signifying "sacred" narrative and re-emplotted in another that leads to Hitler. This re-emplotment deprives the events of their prestige, their aura, rendering them easier to challenge.

Weil's treatment of the prevalent narrative constitutes a thoroughgoing and effective dismantling of it. Once the sacred history is weakened, it can no longer be seen as robust enough to embody the "shared meaning" of the community. Weil's treatment represents an act of resistance. As Robyn Fivush writes,

> When the narrative is contested, there is a perception that one narrative cannot be "right" whereas the other narrative is, and, critically, the "right" narrative carries the moral imperative. . . . This is how resistance narratives can create change: through claiming the moral imperative, resistance narratives challenge the truth, not the accuracy, of culturally dominant narratives.[78]

"To love France, it's necessary to feel she has a past, but it's not necessary to love the historical envelope of this past,"[79] Weil asserts. Even if the past is a treasure, essential to the nourishment of the French comity, its emplotment as narrative history might be more harmful than useful. Weil proposes discarding this husk. As she has shown, there are dangers inherent in any official national history: the necessary selection and omission of event; the proven danger of using an historical narrative to structure and later manipulate a people. Even these dangers are less objectionable to her, perhaps, than the fact that historical narrative arranges the past on a horizontal vector that moves inexorably forward, from "less good" to "better," enshrining the concept of progress. The emphasis on progress represents for Weil a laicization of the concept of redemption, transforming it into "a temporal rather than an eternal operation."[80] Susan Neiman's description of the post-Enlightenment appropriation of sacred history encapsulates Weil's assessment: "One's history was a matter of consolation or pride: *just see how far we've come from barbarism* [emphasis in original]. . . . The modern subject of history evolved as a substitute for Providence. . . . Hence history was studied for signs of progress within it."[81]

A corollary of this misappropriation of redemption to "sacralize" secular constructs, in Weil's view, is the fact that the "dogma of progress" leads to a moral relativism. After she has refused Saint Louis admission into the small sample of admirable figures in French history due to his attitude toward heretics, she imagines the objections that might be raised: "It was the spirit of his time, which, being situated seven centuries before ours, was proportionately clouded."[82] She terms this assertion "a lie." What is evil is so in all times and in all places. "The dogma of progress dishonors the good in making it a question of fashion."[83]

So it is not just France's particular arrangement of the past as narrative that Weil rejects. Her objection is much more thoroughgoing. The primary Free French project should be the fashioning of a "soul" for France, and the soul belongs to God. In "Reflections Without Order Concerning the Love of God," she poses the following conundrum: "How can we seek God, since he is above, in the dimension we travel? We can only walk horizontally."[84] She rejects categorically the entire concept of a past imagined as a horizontal vector *toward* some good.

Weil offers an alternate model for the past that would abandon any concept of a signifying narrative: all the "data" of French history, its events and its actors, would exist disconnected from a plot line that tells a single story with a teleological thrust. All these elements would instead constitute what she terms the *milieu vital*, "vital medium":

> In defining the fatherland as a certain *milieu vital* one avoids the contradictions and lies which corrode patriotism. It is one *milieu vital*, but there are others. It was produced by a tangle of causes where the good and the bad are mixed together, the just and unjust, and due to this fact it is not the best possible. It was perhaps constituted at the expense of another combination richer in vital properties (*effluves*), and in the case that is true, regrets would be legitimate; but past events are done; this milieu exists, and such as it is must be preserved as a treasure for the good it contains.[85]

Weil presents this *milieu vital* in a decidedly non-narrative way. It is propelled by no initial situation; it appears accidental rather than necessary; it shows no teleological design or satisfying closure; the forces motoring it are mixed at best; and the causes are tangled rather than growing logically from and leading to others in a more linear fashion.

This *milieu vital* abandons the metaphor of the past strung upon a horizontal line; it brings to mind instead a liquid-filled sphere (*effluves*). In this sphere, Joan of Arc and the inhabitants of Béziers float cheek to jowl next to Napoleon and Richelieu; Rabelais and Racine are in suspension next to the merely talented Corneille and Lamartine; the Romanesque churches in the South of France testify to the richness of the Cathar culture, bumping up against the crushing of the Commune. What is pure, middling, evil all float suspended in the same medium. Logical cause and effect, selection and omission, narrative frameworks and endpoints have liquesced in its viscous growth medium. If, as Weil states, "To love France, it is necessary to feel that it has a past," it would require an apprenticeship in *lecture*, reading, for her compatriots to love France through the shapeless, random jumble of the *milieu vital*. Pried from their narrative setting, Weil invites us to consider the elements of the past in a different way. Rather than pulling us forward on a horizontal of secular redemption, they can, so considered, pull our attention vertically, to God. They can act as *metaxu*, a bridge between the universe and God.

It is easy to imagine some of the elements in this milieu serving that purpose. Weil asks if it is not possible to agree to admire only those actions and lives that emit "the spirit of truth, justice and love,"[86] those things in history that have shown themselves "perfectly pure."[87] These goods partake of the beauty of the world, which can act as *metaxu* if approached not as ends in themselves but as an orientation to God. They are unfortunately rare; because the prevalent historical narrative has displaced them and largely erased their traces, they are "inarticulate, anonymous," and have "vanished."[88] There are very few examples accessible; Weil evokes Joan of Arc, moved by her "pity" for France to lead forces against the English invaders and ensure France was led by a consecrated king; the Cathars, the "heretical" sect destroyed in the Crusades against it; the citizens of Béziers who refused to hand over their Cathar neighbors to the swords of the invading French. Despite the paucity of examples, Weil insists:

> If there are geniuses whose genius is pure to the point of being manifestly close to the greatness befitting the most perfect of saints, why waste time admiring others? We can make use of those others, draw knowledge and pleasure from them; but why love them? Why give one's heart to anything other than the good?[89]

Other elements are harder to imagine as bridges toward God. After all, this *milieu vital* will still include the Crusades against the Cathars, and, more recent, the Debacle and the Occupation. It is more of a challenge to see these as *metaxu*, as objects of attention that can orient us upward. But their very difficulty, their function as stumbling blocks, makes them valuable. To understand how Weil is recasting the "soul" of France through this newly imagined past, it is helpful to turn to her essays on religion, in particular "Forms of the Implicit Love of God" and "The Love of God and Affliction."

Weil invites her compatriots to approach, through the past, the universe "as it is"—not "improved" by narrative or by omissions or hypertrophy of certain elements. The order of the world is constituted by necessity, and, in contradistinction to an end-oriented narrative, has no "intention and finality."[90] To relinquish those concepts is to unhook oneself from comforting but limiting moorings.

Necessity is the "trace" God left in the world when he withdrew from creation to leave space for human activity. His retreat is a sign not of His indifference but of His love. In coming to accept the past "such as it is," not amenable to control by human fashioning, not moving toward a secular salvation, with no consoling function, we have the opportunity to approach God by accepting the necessity that is the footprint He left in creation. This necessity can include that most devastating of encounters, that with *malheur*, affliction. "We must tenderly love the hardness of this necessity, which is like a two-sided medal, the side turned toward us being domination, the side turned toward God being obedience."[91] If Weil jettisoned the concept of providential history and secular salvation history, she has not for all that abandoned the concepts of either Providence or salvation. But this Providence intended necessity to be a "blind mechanism."[92] Rather than existing in the horizontal of cause and effect, the elements ruled by this hard necessity point upward, orienting us on what Christy Wampole calls "the vertical sacred," "a concrete, spiritually infused world."[93]

So in France's history seen "just as it is," God has left breadcrumbs of grace—the invitation to encounter the adamantine cliff face of necessity's blind mechanisms as well as the examples of purity, love, justice, the saints. All can serve as traces that lead to Him.

This reader of Weil has focused on narrative, both in her academic life and outside of it. I rely on narrative sense-making to order experience, to minimize chaos, and to impose meaning on the seemingly accidental. From what we've looked at in the preceding chapters, Weil's compatriots of 1943 would have shared my predilections. They grew up sharing a certain collective memory, were educated into a certain understanding of their past, and took much of their identity from both. And perhaps the claim of narrative psychologists that *all* human knowledge is narrative can be qualified to the more modest assertion that *much* human knowledge is narrative.

Given this, I can't but stand in admiration at the audacity of Weil's project. She used her rich knowledge of French "official history" and her familiarity with its strategies to blow it up completely. She worked to detach her compatriots from a familiar, comforting but distorting vision of the order of the world. She invited them to embark on another reading of the past, one that would require an arduous apprenticeship and few recognizable consolations. But she could not do otherwise. Her compatriots had already gorged on lies and murk. She would not add to them by pandering with half-truths.

NOTES

1. "Mots qui soulagent mais qui disloquent tout ce qui reste encore de solide (si peu, il est vrai) dans l'armature sociale et militaire de la France."

Henri Amouroux, *Grande Histoire des Français sous l'occupation*, Vol. I: Le Peuple du désastre (Paris: Robert Laffont, 1976), 490.

2. Pierre Laborie, *L'Opinion française sous Vichy* (Paris: Seuil, 1990), 236.

3. There are certain kinds of text that this discussion will not treat—works of imaginative literature; memoirs or personal journals meant for more private analysis than directed at informing public discourse; "belletristic" chronicles or memoirs of the war, such as Henri de Montherlant's *Solstice de juin*, a series of short essays where he merely "improvises" on the war to explore his own reactions to it.

4. Stanley Hoffmann has called Bloch, Blum, and De Gaulle's treatments the "three greats" in view of the comprehensive analysis they give of the Debacle. He refers to De Gaulle's *Mémoires de guerre* rather than his addresses made during the war, but the assessments of the defeat are similar in both. "The Trauma of 1940: A Disaster and Its Traces," in *The French Defeat of 1940: Reassessments*, ed. Joel Blatt (Providence, Berghahn Books, 1998), 356.

5. Jean Weiland, *Pourquoi nous croyons en la collaboration*, Talk given Dec. 27, 1940 (Paris: Groupe Collaboration, 1940), 27.

6. "Toutes les propagandes du monde ne prevaudront pas contre cette évidence: l'Angleterre a perdu la guerre comme nous le 18 mai 1940.

Qu'elle résiste plus ou moins longtemps aux bombardements, qu'elle cherche à déplacer, en Afrique ou ailleurs, le champs de bataille, ceci ne change rien à la situation en Europe. L'Europe se refait sans l'Angleterre."

Weiland, *Pourquoi*, 21.

7. "D'un côté, deux cent cinquante millions d'habitants, dont vingt millions de soldats, vivant sur les terres les plus riches et les plus civilisées du Vieux Monde. De l'autre, trente-trois millions d'êtres, dont une moitié sauvages, sur les territoires aux trois quarts désertiques gardés par cinquante ou soixante mille soldats.

Les bons peuples libéraux d'Occident n'en attendent pas moins avec une confiance souriante le prochain triomphe des démocraties.

Laissons un instant ces doux idiots."

Lucien Rebatet, *Les Décombres* (Paris: Denoel, 1942), 541.

8. "La faillite morale des années d'avant-guerre"

Jean Thouvenin, *La France Nouvelle.* V. 1, 2, 4 and 5 (Paris: Sequana, 1940), 7.

9. "l'esprit de jouissance," "l'esprit de sacrifice"

Thouvenin, *La France*, 9.

10. "fonctionnaires tarés, politiciens néfastes, instituteurs bornés, syndicats, agents des loges et des ghettos, financiers véreux."

Weiland, *Pourquoi*, 38.

11. "la France juive et démocratique encanaillée, décervelée, burlesque."

Rebatet, *Les Décombres*, 476.

12. "La première condition était pour nous de liquider absolument notre passé . . . Pour les institutions vermoulues du régime, à qui nous n'avions même pas été fichus de donner le coup de grâce, les Panzer-divisionen avaient tout jeté par terre. Il ne nous restait plus qu'à pousser les morceaux à la charognerie."

Rebatet, *Les Décombres*, 476.

13. "une manie presque perverse de flagellation volontaire."

Léon Blum, *A l'Echelle humaine*, in *L'Oeuvre de Léon Blum 1940–1945* (Paris: Albin Michel, 1955), 412. https://gallica.bnf.fr/ark:/12148/bpt6k20641m/f1.item.

14. Blum, *A l'Echelle*, 413.

15. Blum, *A l'Echelle*, 411–12.

16. Marc Bloch, *L'Étrange Défaite. Témoignage écrit en 1940. Suivi de Écrits clandestins 1942-44* (Paris: Albin Michel, 1957), 50.

17. "nos chefs, au milieu de beaucoup de contradictions, ont prétendu, avant tout, renouveller, en 1940, la guerre de 1915–1918. Les Allemands faisaient celle de 1940."
   Bloch, *L'Étrange Défaite*, 81.
18. "Face a une armée allemande, débarrassée de toutes les références, moderne dans sa technique aussi bien que dans sa pensée stratégique, nos journaux, nos généraux, nos ministres, jusqu'à la fin tragique, s'accrochent toujours aux souvenirs de 1914–1918, comme s'il était possible de plagier le courage, le success, la gloire."
   Amoureux, *Grande histoire*, Vol. 1, 289.
19. Bloch, *L'Etrange Défaite*, 62.
20. Bloch, *L'Etrange Défaite*, 76.
21. Bloch, *L'Etrange Défaite*, 81.
22. "Nous venons de subir une incroyable défaite. À qui la faute? Au régime parlementaire, à la troupe, aux Anglais, à la cinquième colonne, répondent nos généraux. À tout le monde, en somme, sauf à eux."
   Bloch, *L'Etrange Défaite*, 49.
23. "Ils n'ont accepté le désastre que la rage au coeur. Ils l'ont accepté, cependant, trop tôt, parce qu'ils lui trouvaient ces atroces consolations: écraser, sous les ruines de la France, un régime honni: plier les genoux devant le châtiment que le destin avait envoyé à une nation coupable."
   Bloch, *L'Etrange Défaite*, 214.
24. "L'historien . . . sait bien que deux guerres qui se suivent, si, dans l'intervalle, la structure sociale, les techniques, la mentalité se sont métamorphosées, ne seront jamais la même guerre."
   Bloch, *L'Etrange Défaite*, 157.
25. "À vrai dire, que les partis qualifiés de 'droite' soient si prompts aujourd'hui à s'incliner devant la défaite, un historien ne saurait en éprouver une bien vive surprise. Telle a été presque tout au long de notre destin leur constante tradition: depuis la Restauration jusqu'à l'assemblée de Versailles."
   Bloch, *L'Etrange Défaite*, 193.
26. "source profonde."
   Bloch, *L'Etrange Défaite*, 210.
27. "authentique patrimoine."
   Bloch, *L'Etrange Défaite*, 221.
28. "Il est deux catégories de Français qui ne comprendront jamais l'histoire de France, ceux qui refusent de vibrer au souvenir du sacre de Reims; ceux qui lisent sans émotion le récit de la fête de la Fédération. Peu importe l'orientation présente de leurs préférences. Leur imperméabilité aux plus beaux jaillissements de l'enthousiasme collectif suffit à les condamner."
   Bloch, *L'Etrange Défaite*, 210.
29. "prétendus apôtres de la tradition."
   Bloch, *L'Etrange Défaite*, 220.
30. Bloch, *L'Etrange Défaite*, 190.
31. "le plus atroce effondrement."
   Bloch, *L'Etrange Défaite*, 21.

32. Carol Fink, *Marc Bloch: A Life in History* (New York: Cambridge University Press, 1989), 240.

33. Hilary Footit and John Simmonds, "Destroying the Myths of Debacle," *Durham French Studies* 3 (1991): 24.

34. "impréparation de la guerre en France de 1936–1940."

Significantly, the inquiry into the "impréparation de la guerre en France de 1936–1940" was to reach back no further than March of 1936. And, again significantly, it pursued those responsible for the lack of preparation for the war rather than those most closely associated with its lost battles. This delimitation ensured, first of all, that certain figures important in the Vichy regime would be protected from scrutiny, specifically Pétain, a major figure within the military between the wars and minister of war in 1934, and Weygand, who had been the commander in chief of the Armed Forces at the armistice. It also allowed the court to include Léon Blum among the accused (he served as prime minister from June 1936 to June of 1937).

35. "d'avoir manqué aux devoirs de leur charge dans la période critique où ils étaient au pouvoir."

36. "Messieurs, j'ai achevé. Vous pourrez naturellement nous condamner. Je crois que, même par votre arrêt, vous ne pourrez pas effacer notre oeuvre. Je crois que vous ne pourrez pas—le mot vous paraîtra peut-être orgueilleux—nous chasser de l'histoire de ce pays. Nous n'y mettons pas de présomption, mais nous y apportons une certaine fierté: nous avons dans un temps bien périlleux, personnifié et vivifié la tradition authentique de notre pays, qui est la tradition démocratique et républicaine. De cette tradition, à travers l'histoire, nous aurons malgré tout été un moment. Nous ne sommes pas je ne sais quelle excroissance monstrueuse dans l'histoire de ce pays, parce que nous avons été un gouvernement populaire; nous sommes dans la tradition de ce pays depuis la Révolution française. Nous n'avons pas interrompu la chaîne, nous ne l'avons pas brisée, nous l'avons renouée et nous l'avons resserrée."

Léon Blum, *Devant la cour de Riom février-mars 1942* (Paris : Éditions de la liberté, 1945), 200–201.

37. "Qui sait? D'ici un siècle ou deux, quand les penseurs envisageront avec une parfaite sérénité le développement de notre âge, peut-être iront-ils jusqu'à juger que le nazisme et le fascisme ont eux-mêmes joué leur rôle dans cette marche providentielle du progrès."

Blum, *Devant la cour*, 222.

38. Charles De Gaulle, *Appels et discours 1940–1943* (n.p., 1943), 37.

39. "Vous qui avez présidé à notre organisation militaire après la guerre 1914–1918, vous qui fûtes Généralissime jusqu'en 1932 . . . Vous qui fûtes Ministre de la Guerre en 1938, vous qui étiez la plus haute personnalité militaire de notre pays, avez-vous jamais soutenu, demandé, exigé, la réforme indispensable de ce système?"

De Gaulle, *Appels et discours*, 12–13.

40. "Cet excès de douleur et cet abandon feraient le jeu de nos ennemis."

"Le slogan d'une France pécheresse, justement punie de ses fautes et qui court à l'expiation, voilà qui convient tout à fait à nos vainqueurs du moment. Voilà qui répond trop bien aux remords et aux intérêts de ceux qui ont capitulé."

De Gaulle, *Appels et discours*, 18.

41. "Jeanne d'Arc, Richelieu, Louis XIV, Carnot, Napoléon, Gambetta, Poincaré, Clémenceau, le Maréchal Foch auraient-ils jamais consenti à livrer toutes les armes de la France à ses ennemis pour qu'ils puissent s'en servir contre les Alliés?

Que de bons Français se posent ces questions. Ils comprendront aussitôt où est l'honneur, où est l'intérêt, où est le bon sens."

De Gaulle, *Appels et discours*, 16.

42. "Les gens qui s'étonnent de ne pas trouver parmi nous des politiciens usés, des académiciens somnolents, des hommes d'affaires manégés par les combinaisons, des généraux épuisés de grades, font penser à ces attardés des petites cours d'Europe qui, pendant la dernière révolution française, s'offusquaient de ne pas voir siéger Turgot, Necker et Laménie de Brienne au Comité de Salut Public. Que voulez-vous? Une France en révolution préfère toujours gagner la guerre avec le Général Hoche plutôt que de la perdre avec le Maréchal de Soubise. Pour proclamer et imposer la Déclaration des Droits une France en révolution préfère toujours écouter Danton plutôt que de s'endormir aux ronrons des formules d'autrefois."

De Gaulle, *Appels et discours*, 69–70.

43. "la somme énorme des mérites et des vertus de la France"

De Gaulle, *Appels et discours*, 37.

44. Stanley Hoffmann terms this analysis the Gaullist "simple and archetypal frame of the Fall, followed by the Call and the long collective ascent toward Unity and Salvation."

"The Trauma of 1940," 362.

45. De Gaulle, *Appels et discours*, 76.

46. Andrew Shennen, *Rethinking France: Plans for Renewal, 1940–1946* (New York: Oxford University Press, 1989), 37.

47. The analyses of the Debacle outlined so far fit neatly within the four thematic historiographical approaches to the Fall of France laid out by the historian Richard Carswell: decadence, failure, constraint, and contingency. The voices from the far right clearly call up the theme of "decadence"; Bloch's study pointedly focuses on the failures or poor decisions made by the higher echelons of the military; Blum and DeGaulle both point out the contingencies responsible for the defeat, the military missteps responsible for losing the battle of France.

Richard Carswell, *The Fall of France in the Second World War: History and Memory* (Palgrave Macmillan, 2019).

48. Nicholas Atkin, *Church and Schools in Vichy France, 1940–1944* (New York: Garland Pub. Inc., 1991).

Robert Paxton, *Vichy France: Old Guard and New Order, 1940–1944* (New York: Knopf, 1972).

Gordon Wright, *Rural Revolution in France: The Peasantry in the Twentieth Century* (Stanford: Stanford University Press, 1964).

Shennen, *Rethinking France*.

49. Not surprisingly, the greatest investment in time and effort was put into expelling from the profession those teachers too vocally supportive of Republicanism and then censoring, revising and developing new history textbooks in an effort to eradicate the Republican version and substitute for it the Vichy version.

Debbie Lackerstein, *National Regeneration in Vichy France: Ideas and Policies, 1930–1944* (Burlington, VT: Ashgate, 2012), 178–79.

50. Not all were abandoned after the war. Gordon Wright argues that certain Vichy agrarian initiatives took root and served as the basis for the postwar period: the *Corporations paysannes* produced a new cadre of agrarian leaders bringing with them modernizing ideas such as bringing in technical aide to lower production costs and the cooperative use of farm machinery (Wright 87–90). Paxton traces the impact of the technical and economic specialists associated with *École Nationale des cadres d'Uriage* and the "industrial rationalization and concentration" and economic planning of the postwar period that ushered in *les Trente glorieuses*, that period of exponential growth of the economy and living standards (Paxton 354–55).

51. Wright, *Rural Revolution*; Shennen, *Rethinking France*,

52. "on aurait pu croire que la France n'avait commencé à connaître la gloire, la prosperité, qu'après la Révolution, et qu'il n'y avait avant que misère, ténèbres et guerres. On effaçait ainsi quinze siècles d'histoire, des siècles comme le XIIIe ou le XVII, où la France connut une prosperité et un prestige incomparables dans le monde."

Qtd. in Nicholas Atkin, *Church and Schools in Vichy France, 1940–1944* (New York: Garland, 1991), 70.

53. Atkin, *Church and Schools*, 71, 72.

54. See preceding chapter and Atkin, *Church and Schools*, 74.

55. "Ce numéro est dédié à ceux qui ont lutté, *par tous les moyens*, contre la barbarie révolutionnaire, et, particulièrement, aux PAYSANS VENDÉENS morts pour la vérité, aussi qu'à la haute et sainte mémoire de Charlotte de Corday."

Je Suis Partout. Numéro dédié à la Révolution. No. 449 (30 juin 1939). https://www.retronews.fr/journal/je-suis-partout/30-juin-1939/719/2125577/1?from=%2Fsearch%23sort%3Dscore%26publishedBounds%3Dfrom%26indexed-Bounds%3Dfrom%26tfPublications%255B0%255D%3DJe%2520suis%2520partout%26page%3D19%26searchIn%3Dall%26total%3D683&index=449.

56. Léon Daudet, *Les Lys sanglants: roman historique* (Paris: Flammarion, 1938).

57. "Si violent fût-il, le refus des contre-révolutionnaires se tient d'ailleurs dans les limites du verbe. Pour qu'il se transformât en riposte, il aurait fallu que Louis XIV, Racine ou Olivier de Serres, sans parler de Grégoire de Tours, célébrés dans les cercles les plus conservateurs, fissent poids de mémoire en face de 89."

Pascal Ory, *Une Nation pour memoire: 1889, 1939, 1989. Trois jubilés révolutionnaires* (Paris: Presses de la Fondation Nationale des Sciences Politiques, 1992), 182.

58. "Léon Daudet, dans ses charmants *Souvenirs*, constate avec bonhomie qu'il aurait suffi, à chaque crise de la République, d'un général, voire d'un colonel résolu à un acte d'énergie pour que le régime passât de vie à trépas. C'est au moins vraisemblable, si l'on songe à l'équipe de ce malheureux imbécile de Boulanger qui n'avait pas cinq cents mètres à faire, de la Madeleine à l'Élysée, pour devenir le maître de la France, et qui n'osa pas les faire."

Rebatet, *Les Décombres*, 572.

59. "réactiver 'aux yeux de tous' . . . un des éléments de sa légitimité, le plus souvent un événement ou une figure fondateurs, l'objectif étant la constitution d'un consensus rétrospectif."

Ory, *Une Nation pour mémoire*, 8.

60. "Et je cherche en vain une raison quelconque au nom de laquelle je devrais chérir moins fraternellement mes camarades allemands, connus et inconnus, que n'importe quels Français."

Qtd. in Simone Pétrement, *La Vie de Simone Weil* 1 (Paris: Fayard, 1973), 341.

61. "[Les Français] savent qu'une partie de leur âme colle tellement à la France que lorsque la France leur est ôtée, elle y reste collée, comme la peau d'un objet brûlant, et est ainsi arrachée."

Simone Weil, *L'Enracinement: Prélude à une déclaration des devoirs envers l'être humain*, *OC* V, Vol. 2 (Paris: Gallimard, 2013), 241.

62. Diane de Bellescize, "Le Comité general d'études de la Résistance," *Revue d'histoire de la Deuxième Guerre mondiale*, 25e Année, No. 99, Aspects de la Resistance française (Juillet 1975): 1–24.

63. Simone Weil, "Légitimité du gouvernement provisoire," in *OC* V, Vol. 3 (Paris: Gallimard, 2019), 389.

64. In this view she was anticipated by drafters of the French Constitution of 1789—a heated exchange took place on whether a constitution could be drawn up without having a statement of philosophical principles that could inform and justify the articles. The Declaration of Rights of Man and the Citizen in 1789 preceded the drafting of the constitution.

Keith Michael Baker, *Inventing the French Revolution: Essays on French Political Culture in the 18th Century* (New York: Cambridge University Press, 1990), 251.

65. The working groups of *la France combattante* were deliberating another such declaration titled "Déclaration des droits et des devoirs de l'homme et du citoyen" ("Declaration of the Rights and Obligations of Man and the Citizen") at approximately the same time. Significantly, the constitution of the postwar Fourth Republic, approved in 1946, refers to "des droits inaliénables et sacrés," "les droits et libertés de l'homme et du citoyen consacrés par la Déclaration des droits de 1789" ("inalienable and sacred rights," "the rights and freedoms of man and the citizen consecrated by the Declaration of Rights of 1789"), omitting the notion of "obligations" entirely.

66. Mamadi Keita reminds the reader of a different kind of rights introduced in the Constitution of 1848: "Désormais, on n'attend plus de l'État qu'il se borne à garantir les droits politiques de l'individu, mais qu'il intervienne dans la vie politique et sociale de la nation pour créer des opportunités ou corriger des inegalités." ("From that point on, one no longer expects the State to limit itself to guaranteeing the individual's political rights, but to intervene in the political and social life of the nation to create opportunities or redress inequalities.") These rights do not merely constitute "bornes" but entail obligations to the human being.

Mamadi Keita, "Critique de L'état-nation dans 'l'Enracinement' de Simone Weil," *CLA Journal* 46, no. 4 (June 1, 2003): 554. https://search-ebscohost-com.ezproxyles.flo.org/login.aspx?direct=true&AuthType=cookie,ip&db=edsjsr&AN=edsjsr.44325183&site=eds-live&scope=site.

67. Baker, *Inventing*, 267.
68. Baker, *Inventing*, 267.
69. "Il y a là une responsabilité terrible. Car il s'agit de ce qu'on appelle refaire une âme au pays; et il y a une si forte tentation de la refaire à coups de mensonges ou de vérités partielles qu'il faut plus que de l'héroïsme pour s'attacher à la vérité."
    Weil, *L'Enracinement*, 233.
70. "C'est un peuple qui a ouvert la main et laissé la patrie tomber par terre."
    Weil, *L'Enracinement*, 193.
71. "Donner aux Français quelque chose à aimer. Et leur donner d'abord à aimer la France. Concevoir la réalité correspondante au nom de France de telle manière que telle qu'elle est, dans sa vérité, elle puisse être aimée avec toute l'âme."
    Weil, *L'Enracinement*, 239.
72. "nous ne possédons d'autre vie, d'autre sève, que les trésors hérités du passé et digérés, assimilés, recréés par nous. De tous les besoins de l'âme humaine, il n'y en a pas de plus vital que le passé."
    Weil, *L'Enracinement*, 150.
73. Weil, *L'Enracinement*, 269.
74. "état de stupeur," "rongés," "chair à canon"
    Weil, *L'Enracinement*, 148.
75. Weil, *L'Enracinement*, 266.
76. "Évoquer en ce moment la grandeur historique de la France, ses gloires passées et futures, l'éclat dont son existence a été entourée, cela n'est pas possible sans une espèce de raidissement intérieur qui donne au ton quelque chose de forcé. Rien qui ressemble à de l'orgueil ne peut convenir aux malheureux."
    Weil, *L'Enracinement*, 252.
77. "Pour le progrès, pour l'accomplissement de l'Histoire, il faut peut-être en passer par là . . . La France a eu la victoire en 1918; elle n'a pu accomplir l'unité de l'Europe; maintenant l'Allemagne essaie de l'accomplir; ne la gênons pas."
    Weil, *L'Enracinement*, 230.
78. Robyn Fivush, "Speaking Silence: The Social Construction of Silence in Autobiographical and Cultural Narratives," *Memory* 18, no. 2 (February 2010): 95–96. doi: 10.1080/09658210903029404.
79. "Pour aimer la France il faut sentir qu'elle a un passé, mais il ne faut pas aimer l'enveloppe historique de ce passé."
    Weil, *L'Enracinement*, 297.
80. "une conception historique de la Rédemption qui en fait une opération temporelle et non éternelle."
    Weil, *L'Enracinement*, 295.
81. Susan Neiman, *Learning from the Germans: Confronting Race and the Memory of Evil* (London: Allen Lane, 2019), 283.
82. "c'était l'esprit de son temps, lequel, étant situé sept siècles avant le nôtre, était obnubilé en proportion."
    Weil, *L'Enracinement*, 294.
83. "Le dogme du progrès déshonore le bien en le faisant une affaire de mode."
    Weil, *L'Enracinement*, 295.

84. Simone Weil, "Réflexions sans ordre sur l'amour de Dieu," *OC* IV, Vol. 1 (Paris: Gallimard, 2008), 278.

85. "En définissant la patrie comme un certain milieu vital, on évite les contradictions et les mensonges qui rongent le patriotisme. Il est un certain milieu vital; mais il y en a d'autres. Il a été produit par un enchevêtrement de causes où se sont mélangés le bien et le mal, le juste et l'injuste, et de ce fait il n'est pas le meilleur possible. Il s'est peut-être constitué aux dépens d'une autre combinaison plus riche en effluves vitales, et au cas où il en serait ainsi les regrets seraient légitimes; mais les événements passés sont accomplis; ce milieu existe, et tel qu'il est doit être préservé comme un trésor à cause du bien qu'il contient."

Weil, *L'Enracinement*, 243.

86. Weil, *L'Enracinement*, 294.

87. Weil, *L'Enracinement*, 297.

88. Weil, *L'Enracinement*, 297.

89. "S'il y a des génies chez qui le génie est pur au point d'être manifestement tout proche de la grandeur propre au plus parfait des saints, pourquoi perdre son temps à admirer d'autres? On peut user des autres, puiser chez eux des connaissances et des jouissances; mais pourquoi les aimer? Pourquoi accorder son coeur à autre chose qu'au bien?"

Weil, *L'Enracinement*, 300.

90. Weil, "Formes de l'amour implicite de Dieu," *OC* IV, Vol. 1 (Paris: Gallimard, 2008), 312.

91. "Il faut aimer tendrement la dureté de cette nécessité qui est comme une médaille à double face, la face tournée vers nous étant domination, la face tournée vers Dieu étant obéisance."

Weil, "L'Amour de Dieu," 362.

92. "un mécanisme aveugle."

Weil, "L'Amour de Dieu," 352.

93. Christy Wampole, "Saving Europe from Itself: Weil's Enracinement and Heidegger's Bodenständigkeit," in *Rootedness: The Ramifications of a Metaphor* (Chicago: University of Chicago Press, 2016), 13. doi: 10.7208/chicago/9780226317793.003.0005.

In the Way of a Conclusion

In *L'Enracinement* Weil laid out the "fundamental notions" for rebuilding France after the war and proposed a basis for imagining a France that could shine as a beacon. To what degree were her hopes realized in the immediate postwar?

In 1943, *la France combattante* was establishing itself as a settled governing group; Vichy was losing credibility, recognition, adherents, and military effectives; the fortunes of war were turning toward the Allies. These developments gladdened the heart of those who hoped to see Germany go down to defeat; Simone Weil, however, was increasingly locked in despondency and bitterness.[1] She was heartsick to be distant from France and her compatriots suffering under the increasing harshness of German occupation and was bitterly disappointed by the refusal of the London authorities to drop her into France as a clandestine operative. Her disheartenment is in part also attributable to her advancing tuberculosis. But it expresses as well, in my view, her cruel disillusionment toward the postwar France being imagined and scaffolded in London and Algiers.

There was expectation early on in some Resistance circles of a thoroughgoing transformation of France. A reimagined, more just France seemed tantalizingly possible, in particular given the number of communist and socialist *résistants* and the thorough discrediting of the prewar government. And this reimagining of France would not have an impact just within her borders, but in the wider world, as Weil herself had hoped. Although France should no longer presume to "think for the universe," it still held a universal mission.

> Prostrate, stretched out on the ground, still half dead, perhaps nonetheless she can try to begin once again to think about the destiny of the world. Not to decide it, because she has no authority for that. To think it through, that's totally different.[2]

These hopes and this conviction raised the stakes for what was being deliberated in Free French circles in London—Weil and others had anticipated the possibility of laying the foundations for a France which would serve once again as a model for other peoples.

Skepticism about the possibility for thoroughgoing change was growing in 1943, however, as blueprints for France's future took shape. That year, a *Comité Général d'Études* questionnaire was sent out widely to Resistance circles to get feedback on the proposals being entertained. One respondent from a network in the south of France expresses the concerns of many: France's opportunity for a fundamental reshaping is fading. None of what he has seen so far in the circulated papers gives him confidence that his own core concern will be addressed: the establishment of a "greater social justice."[3] This writer would have found a sympathetic ear in Simone Weil.

It is perhaps understandable that *la France combattante* would opt for what was recognizable and would fall back on structures that were familiar. Its first objective was maintaining a united front in pursuit of the war and victory—all else ceded to this aim. Coming down on one side or another of important policy issues before victory, given the number of political factions and ideologies uncomfortably housed in the Free French big tent, could jeopardize that primary goal. As Andrew Shennen remarks, "Disunity was regarded as the ultimate sacrilege and it was recognized that defining specific programmes—in other words making unambiguous political choices—would inevitably produce splits."[4] Stability and order seemed a preferable option to the longer churn that more thoroughgoing change would require.

In the end, the constitution of the Fourth Republic, although giving the president more decision-making authority in order to preclude the dizzying change of governments that marked the interwar period (a goal it did *not* achieve), did not differ strikingly from that of the Third Republic,[5] a constitution that, in Weil's view, was so unloved that the French people saw it trammeled in 1940 with little emotion.[6] And although the proposals for political parties had included one for a single party growing out of resistance groups (Weil termed these plans for a single party "fascist"[7]), what emerged was, likewise, not dramatically different from what preceded the Debacle, with the Communist Party, Socialist Party, and the MRP (*Mouvement républicaine populaire*), to which conservative and Catholic voters flocked, standing in the first postwar elections. Vichy's policies and initiatives were to be abrogated or dismantled out of hand, a point Weil disagreed with. She gives a fair hearing to some she considers valid: the push to revivify regional identification, the policies that aimed at emphasizing the importance of agrarian life and farming, the focus on communitarian life, and the salutary study of sacred texts in schools.[8]

The issue with which she most strongly takes issue is France's continuing identity as an imperial power. Although a "federal" union between France and her colonies had at one time been among the proposals under consideration in a working group of *la France combattante*, with self-government by the colonies and full French citizenship for indigenous peoples, the *Union française* included in the Constitution of 1946 granted white minorities special representation and clearly demonstrated France's intention to prevent any part of the empire from seceding.[9] Weil had argued against granting a special role in colonial affairs to colonists given the understandable distrust toward them among the indigenous peoples.[10]

Her disappointment in some figures who were most closely allied with De Gaulle added to her disillusionment: at the last visit Maurice Schumann made to her sickbed, she refused to speak to him or accept the gift he offered—he was not "sérieux," in her view.[11] Given the pronounced collaborator baiting in his *Radio Londres* programs broadcast to France,[12] she believed he was laying the ground for a campaign of summary justice after the war. She saw concerning signs in the plans for the postwar era, and in this last instance she was most particularly prescient.

Weil foresaw the treatment that would be meted out to those deemed to have collaborated. The "Legal Purge" *(épuration)*, the term given to the process of bringing "traitors" to justice at the end of the war, took place between 1945 and 1949, with the most important of the trials, those of Pétain, the head of state, and Pierre Laval, the prime minister during the greater part of the occupation, taking place in 1945. She understood the longer-term strategic import of this process: the separating of the sheep from the goats, that is, "collaborators" from "patriots."

The speed with which De Gaulle's provisional government dispatched these trials was presented as a necessity: "Justice is not severe unless it is rapid."[13] The precipitous pace of this exercise of justice (indeed one of the major critiques of the process) represented an effort to draw, as quickly as possible, a definitive line after Vichy. In the view of the provisional government, only after having buried that near past would it be possible to construct the future, and any prolonged self-examination was considered a stumbling block to that main goal.

The propaganda broadcasts during the war years into France by *Radio Londres*, an organ of Free France and *la France combattante*, coined the moniker "anti-France"; "France," innocent victim, stands out against "anti-France," its traitorous dark double.[14] This dyad drew a clear demarcation between French "patriots" and French "traitors." This distinction was legally affirmed by a new crime that carried a new punishment. In 1944, the offense of *Indignité nationale* or "national indignity" was created by decree as a way to punish those who had collaborated with the occupying power. In the words of the architects of this law, "But the principle of equality before the law does not oppose the nation making a distinction between good and bad citizens."[15] The sanctions imposed could include deprivation of civic rights, either permanently or for a limited time, a loss of professional position, the confiscation of property.

Weil had foreseen and warned against the danger of assuming the "purity" of some and "impurity" of others. Such a distinction, while perhaps being reassuring in that it "quarantines" bad players, obscures the reality that degrees of complicity defined the life of all of those who lived under occupation.

In a letter Weil wrote from New York to her friend Jean Wahl in 1942, she lays out the large number of possible motives for working with the enemy, not all of which constitute treason. She considers that she herself, as well as most other French, shares some responsibilities for the occupation in their acceptance of the armistice, which cannot be shunted off to a few "traitors."

> I don't much like to hear people who are perfectly comfortable here treat as cowards and traitors those in France who get by as they can in a terrible situation. It is only a small number of French for whom it's fairly certain these adjectives might be deserved; we shouldn't apply them beyond that number. . . . We should only use the word traitor to designate those who one is certain desire the victory of Germany and do what they can to that end. As for the others, some of those who are willing to work with Vichy, and even with the Germans, can have honorable motives corresponding to specific situations. Others can be the object of pressure such that they could not resist without heroism. But most of those who set themselves up as judges here have never had the opportunity to test if they themselves are heroes.[16]

"Guilt," for Weil, proves far more complex than any division of the French into two categories. Justice, and this is after all the question at hand, rests upon discriminations. Without knowing a person's "honorable motives" or "determinate situations," in short, without having plumbed the lived experience of those under accusation, justice goes about her task obstinately blind.

The possibility of charging someone with having worked too closely with the occupation powers put a useful tool in the hands of the new government, however. It provided the means to charge a limited number of people with traitorous acts during wartime. Those so accused and punished serve a salutary purpose: once they are identified, punished, and placed outside the comity, the nation can close ranks and rediscover unity in opposition to them. Its values and its identity are affirmed through the act of expulsion. France was able to "designate the pure and the impure in the same movement, to eliminate the bad French but also to recompose a collective identity."[17] In this context, "purge" is a suggestive term. It implies the elimination of noxious elements, including an "impure" population, from the body politic. In addition, it implies the erasure of all that is impure from the historical memory. It is significant that until the 1970s few studies by French historians addressed the defeat of 1940 and its aftermath.[18] The emphasis was instead on the "resisting" nation that arose to redeem the defeat.[19]

Weil had warned against the dangers posed by burying part of France's history, even those most painful moments. For the Bretons, the Provençaux, and the Corsicans, the tragedies of their present situation could be traced back to a past that was repressed for reasons of state.[20] Drawing a line after trauma does not constitute healing. Henry Rousso traces the pernicious aftermath of France's failure to come to terms with the defeat and occupation. He labels it the Vichy Syndrome.

Rousso discusses France's "repressed trauma" in psychoanalytic terms, which he insists he is using as a metaphor, not "an explanatory system."[21] He divides France's postwar responses into four stages: "mourning," "resistancialism" ("real" France during wartime as entirely aligned with the Resistance), "the return of the repressed," and "obsession." The mourning phase directly after the war, all too perfunctory, gave way speedily to a period of "repression," when "real" France was wholly identified with "resisting" France, which gave no opportunity for a true reckoning with the war, the divisions among the French it had uncovered and the harm the French had inflicted upon each other. In addition, large parts of the population were left out of the "hero" and "traitor" category—those who were deported, the Jews, those conscripted into forced labor for the Germans, the POWs—all erased by this "resistancialist myth."[22] Even the mass amnesties granted in the 1950s to those guilty of collaboration did more to cover up than reconcile; Rousso notes that the word for amnesty in French, "legal oblivion" (*oubli judiciaire*) empowered courts to "impose silence" on all judgments of amnesty.[23]

This teeth-clenching repression shatters during the second cycle of revelations of war crimes and trials of figures such as Paul Touvier, who, as an official of the armed militia (*Milice*), was responsible for a number of extrajudicial killings but who had been pardoned by President Georges Pompidou in an effort to "draw a veil" over the past.[24] In Eric Conan and Henry Rousso's formulation, in this and other long-delayed trials, the past "brutally erupted in the French memory."[25]

In *La Mémoire, l'histoire, l'oubli* (Memory, History, Forgetting) Paul Ricoeur makes no disclaimer about using psychoanalysis as a metaphor rather than an explanatory system. He lays out in psychoanalytic terms the harmful effects of forgetting on a larger community. "The first lesson of psychoanalysis is here that trauma remains even when it is inaccessible, unavailable. In its place arise substitution phenomena, symptoms that mask the return of the repressed under different guises."[26]

Stanley Hoffmann, in his preface to the English translation of the *Vichy Syndrome* in 1991, addresses this admonition to his American audience:

Finally, this book ought to provoke American readers into thinking about their own memories of troubled periods of their past, about evasions, myths, and distortions, and about the way in which the past never ceases to color and to disturb our behavior in the present.[27]

His reminder—or warning—is even more pertinent now than it was 30 years ago.

The issues we've traced in France in the late-nineteenth to mid-twentieth centuries—the competition to define a national "identity"; the struggles to establish an historical narrative that would sacralize that identity; the return of the repressed, or those issues that had been papered over by a narrative rather than faced head-on—are not merely "historical" and quaint, relevant just for France in her past. They all resonate with issues facing the United States in this twenty-first century.

Some unsettling correspondences exist between the two periods: in France prewar, as in the present-day United States, media and press are sharply bifurcated along ideological lines. In France, extreme right wing, Fascist, and anti-Semitic publications competed for readership with the organs of the socialist and communist parties in much the same way as *MSNBC* and *One America News (OAN)*, to say nothing of the echo chamber of social media, represent the extremes of the present-day American political divide.

On February 6, 1934, riots broke out in Paris instigated by far right-wing leagues in what was feared to be a Fascist coup d'état, resulting in the surrounding of the National Assembly. The police successfully put down what was the most serious challenge to the government since the 1871 Commune. In Washington, DC, on January 6, 2021, the Capitol was breeched and occupied in an effort to stop the certification of the 2020 presidential elections and keep Donald Trump in office.

Much like the French of the Third Republic, we speak of Americans' world historical mission, the duty to uphold and spread our own ideals around the world. In a 1998 interview, Madeline Albright, secretary of state to President Bill Clinton, expressed this conviction forcefully. "But if we have to use force, it is because we are America; we are the indispensable nation. We stand tall and we see further than other countries into the future, and we see the danger here to all of us."[28] In 2016, President Obama echoed that choice of words in a speech to the graduating class of West Point.

If the fall of France to a Fascist power called into question its world historical mission, the United States in 2022 finds itself at a similar juncture. America's sacred history, trumpeting the idea that "the arc of the moral universe is long, but it bends toward justice," in Martin Luther King's words, with the powerful American shoulder set to the wheel of that work, is challenged by alternative narratives that call the organizing principle of American history *not* the advancement of liberty and equality, but oppression. And, much like mid-century France, this debate over American exceptionalism is being engaged on the battleground of our history.

Two different documents represent two extreme versions of the historical narratives competing for our attention: The 1619 Project, launched in July 2019 by the *New York Times* as a continuing endeavor, and the Trump Administration's riposte to it, The 1776 Project, released on January 18, 2021. Each project posits a different founding date for the United States—1619, when the first Africans were landed in the colony of Virginia, and 1776, when the Declaration of Independence was adopted by the American colonies. Two starkly different narratives and visions of the future derive from these two dates.

That The 1619 Project offers itself as a "thought experiment," as a *Washington Post* columnist expressed it,[29] is suggested from its opening:

> The goal of The 1619 Project is to reframe American history by considering what it would mean to regard 1619 as our nation's birth year. Doing so requires us to place the consequences of slavery and the contributions of black Americans at the very center of the story we tell ourselves about who we are as a country.[30]

The most controversial element in this account, the claim that has been the object of the most fact-checking and push back from historians of American history, is its recasting of 1776: [31] that slavery constitutes not merely the US "original sin" but "the country's very origin," that the colonies broke with England to *ensure the survival* of the institution, an assertion presented as a commonsense conclusion given the fact that "10 of this nation's first 12 presidents were enslavers."[32]

What ensues is a narrative that places African Americans at its very center, that traces their experiences, primarily, but, as importantly, sees them as central agents in the struggle to realize the principles set forth in the founding documents. No longer mere recipients or beneficiaries of rights secured by others, they are portrayed as the actors who expanded and ensured the rights enjoyed now by all Americans (donor figures, to use formalist terminology). The introductory essay by Nikole Hannah-Jones offers the example of Reconstruction: when African Americans were serving in legislatures in the south, they enacted programs and laws that benefited the entire region, not just their own communities, from the establishment of public schools to passing more equitable tax legislation.[33] After Reconstruction was ended, they themselves were systematically blocked from the enjoyment of the rights and programs they had a hand in creating, while non-African American populations continued to benefit from them.[34]

In addition, the Fourteenth Amendment, passed during Reconstruction, "constitutionally guaranteed equal protection under the law" and had a most significant afterlife. As Hannah-Jones reminds the reader, almost all marginalized groups have used it in their fights for recognition—women, LGBTQ populations, immigrants, and the disabled. In her words, "Through centuries of black resistance and protest, we have helped the country live up to its founding ideals, and not only for ourselves."[35]

In the present day, the writer asserts, efforts by African Americans still power the wheel of the "common good" which is working to reshape America's future: they constitute the strongest supporters of "universal health care and a higher minimum wage," opposition to capital punishment, openness to welcoming more refugees, all of which are in keeping with "the most fundamental of American ideals," and, not surprisingly, constitute an integral part of the Democratic party's program.[36] This hopeful casting of the American future is tempered by doubts that white Americans can serve as reliable partners in the struggle for social justice, given a racism so deep-seated that it might well prove impossible to uproot.[37] However, the choice of an alternate "foundational" event and date (1619) and the shift of Africa Americans from "recipient" to "donor" figures takes apart the familiar narrative of American history and reassembles it.

In November of 2020, President Donald Trump tasked a committee with drawing up The 1776 Project document, a direct riposte to The 1619 Project. It was published on January 18, 2021, two days before the inauguration of Joe Biden, and was withdrawn by order of the new president immediately after his taking office. This document purported to offer what Americans yearn for, "timeless stories and noble heroes that inspire them to be good, brave, diligent, daring, generous, honest and compassionate,"[38] where we can rediscover "our shared identity, rooted in our shared principles."[39]

It is a document that pursues politics by means of an historical narrative, tracing the values and policies of the present-day Republican party back through American history to its founding. By its lights, the second amendment assures the American a right to "his own defense" and is a "check against the worst tyranny";[40] the Progressive movement and the "evolving rights" pursued by its primary figures, Teddy Roosevelt, Woodrow Wilson, and Franklin Roosevelt, are twinned with Fascism in the hypertrophy of "the state," which lives on as an unelected "shadow government";[41] the "right to life" has pride of place alongside civil rights.

It directly engages the claims of The 1619 Project: the founding fathers all "condemned" slavery in "public statements . . . and private letters"[42] and far from framing the constitution in such a way as to ensure the continuation of slavery, they included in it provisions that "planted the seeds of

[its] death."⁴³ Rather than working to ensure the expansion of liberties, the Civil Rights movement lost its way in demanding "affirmative action in the form of preferential treatment"; in so doing, it came close to the white supremacist and segregationist claims of a John Calhoun, who fought for "preferential treatment," but in his case for whites.⁴⁴ While containing "missteps, errors, contradictions, and wrongs," these have all been countered and addressed, and the end result is a history "of self-sacrifice, courage, and nobility."⁴⁵

As was true during the 1939 commemoration of the French Revolution, the battle lines for control of the national historical narrative could not be more clearly drawn, and the present and future premised on these narratives could not stand in greater contrast.

In another symmetry, we in America are undergoing our own version of "the Vichy Syndrome" in that we find ourselves confronted with a past we had previously tried to paper over. Here Henry Rousso offers a pointed reminder:

> There may also be tensions between, on the one hand, the voluntarist "memory" that builds monuments, decorates graves, and buries heroes and, on the other hand, latent or implicit memory, subject to repressions and therefore to slips, lapses, or silences—manifestations of the return of the repressed.⁴⁶

We can see the tensions between "voluntarist" and "implicit" memory in the debate over the place of Civil War monuments in the South. And, as Susan Neiman asserts in *Learning from the Germans: Confronting Race and the Memory of Evil*, "monuments are values made visible."⁴⁷

Neiman reminds the reader that Germany has no statues commemorating Nazis.⁴⁸ A 1945 joint Allied directive barred any monument "which tends to preserve and keep alive the German military tradition" or "is of such a nature to glorify incidents of war."⁴⁹ She compares the US reckoning with slavery to Germany's reckoning with its Nazi past—to the disadvantage of the United States. We find ourselves over 150 years after the Civil War still arguing over the fate of statues celebrating seditionists. Granted, the Allied occupation of West Germany lasted 50 years and included a program to dismantle the Nazi military myth and pursue war criminals, while Reconstruction lasted only 10 years, ending when Rutherford Hayes withdrew Union soldiers from the South in a political arrangement with Southern Democrats to award him the presidency.

Mayor Mitch Landrieu of New Orleans spearheaded an initiative in 2017 to take down four Civil War statues commemorating President of the Confederacy Jefferson Davis, Generals Beauregard and Lee, and the fourth the 1874 Battle of Liberty Place, an attempted coup against the

Reconstructionist state government. Should this decision to take down such monuments be seen as a repression of the past, as some of its opponents have charged?

In a speech laying out the reasons for his decision, Landrieu begins by celebrating the city's diverse peopling, from native to French to African American to Vietnamese. As a sad counterpoint to this diversity, New Orleans was also the site of the largest slave market in the United States, and Louisiana saw numerous lynchings and attacks on Freedom Riders. Why, Landrieu asks, were monuments to the Confederacy erected but none to these other significant events? This is where he identifies historical malfeasance, "a lie by omission."[50] Bryan Stevenson, the executive director of the Equal Justice Initiative and force behind the National Lynching Memorial, posits another equally chilling possibility: "We had a brilliant civil rights movement, but we didn't win the narrative war."[51]

Landrieu reminds his listeners that most Civil War monuments were erected *not* directly after the end of the war but long afterward, in an attempt "to rebrand the history of our city and the ideals of a defeated Confederacy," to "fictionalize" and "sanitize" it.[52] He places the Confederate monuments into a new signifying context, that of the "cult of the lost cause."

The Southern Poverty Law Center determined that by far the greatest number of Civil War monuments to Confederate figures were erected in the early 1900s and late 1950s to early 1960s.[53] These two time periods coincided with, first, the codification of Jim Crow laws that assured resegregation, the separation of the races into "separate but equal" facilities and institutions, as well as the rebirth of the Ku Klux Klan. The second spike coincided with the growing civil rights movement and the passing of early civil rights legislation, which evoked a violent backlash among segregationists. The program of the segregationists in the early 1900s and mid-century was mapped upon, imprinted upon the past, much as we saw the French in 1939 sketch out their national preoccupations and terrors on the canvas of the 150th celebration of the Revolution. In both cases, the "commemoration of the glorious past" revealed much more about the concerns of the present. So rather than "canceling" historical events and figures, Landrieu argues he is reestablishing a more accurate historical context—the "lost cause" was a distortion of history, a reverse image of it. The South lost the war, and soundly, on points and on values, and to remove monuments to the Confederacy does no more than set the record straight.

In addition, Landrieu reminds his listeners, if a reminder is needed, that these monuments were erected to act as objects of terror, a visual reminder of oppression and trauma for African Americans, as much as a burning cross, intended "to send a strong message to all who walked in their shadows about who was still in charge in this city."[54] Simone Weil knew the power of visual reminders; the sight of a German uniform brought back instantly the pain of defeat and occupation to her and her countrymen and had the effect of a blow to the solar plexus.[55]

But while Civil War monuments are being dismantled and moved (albeit in New Orleans under cover of night), other fronts in the battle for the narrative of US history have opened.

Some states and individual school districts have banned any teaching that draws on "Critical Race Theory" (CRT). The group of scholars that represent this school assert that bias and racism exist not only on the level of the individual, that is, not only in those who harbor these biases. Rather, racism is baked into the system in terms of policies enacted, economic incentives and supports bestowed or withheld, and judicial rulings. Racism, the proponents of this school claim, can survive *outside* any individual biased host. In the past, redlining certain neighborhoods made it difficult if not impossible for African Americans to get mortgages; most domestics and sharecroppers, the greater number of whom were African Americans, were blocked from accruing Social Security until 1950; vagrancy laws in the south allowed authorities to press black men into convict labor, reasserting a kind of slavery even after its legal end—all of these policies had pervasive and devastating effects that reach into the present day and all existed outside the mere bias of individuals. CRT argues that present-day American systems are marbled by such a legacy.[56]

Some local and state authorities have passed laws, promulgated executive actions, and approved policies that outlaw the teaching of both Critical Race Theory and The 1619 Project in public schools. Texas law HB No. 3979, signed into law by Governor Abbot in 2021, is transparent in its aims and sets the bar for subsequent policies and legislation. The wording of the law prohibits any curriculum that might suggest any of the following:

> (vi) an individual, by virtue of the individual's race or sex, bears responsibility for actions committed in the past by other members of the same race or sex; (vii) an individual should feel discomfort, guilt, anguish or any other form of psychological distress on account of the individual's race or sex . . . (x) with respect to their relationship with American values, slavery and racism are anything other than deviations from, betrayals of, or failures to live up to, the authentic founding principles of the United States, which include liberty and equality.[57]

Such policies seem intended to extend the "repression" stage of our very own Vichy syndrome, to ensure the wounds that, in Landrieu's words, are "still raw because they never healed right in the first place,"[58] continue to suppurate.

Teaching US history with an eye toward the precepts of CRT or The 1619 Project might, this legislation suggests, elicit feelings of "discomfort" and "guilt" on the part of students. Both "discomfort" and "guilt" are private responses on the part of a solitary individual, and students are supposed to be shielded from experiencing either. Susan Nieman has argued that "guilt" in the face of the historical injustices enacted by one's nation is both insufficient and ineffectual:

> Guilt, it's been argued, is directed inward and no one need know if you have it. Shame, by contrast, is what you feel when you see yourself reflected through others' eyes and you cannot bear to let that image stand. To overcome shame, you must actually do something to show others that you are not inevitably caught in your or your forebears' worst moments.[59]

Shame requires a community, but this legislation suggests that the public arena is no place for reckonings with the past.

The legislation likewise imposes a delimiting narrative frame on the US past: slavery and racism are "deviations" from our "authentic founding principles" rather than integral elements of our history; as mistakes, as errors, as momentary sidetracks, they can be elided. This legislation would keep us immovably enmeshed in the "repression" phase of our own national Vichy syndrome.

The fact that neither of the two documents, The 1619 Project or The 1776 Project, was drafted by professional historians is one of the principal critiques leveled against them. They exist, in this view, as polemical rather than historical arguments. The American historian and public intellectual Jill Lepore cites Carl Degler's pertinent warning: "If we historians fail to provide a nationally defined history, others less critical and less informed will take over the job for us,"[60] and she adds an even more stark warning, "Nations, to make sense of themselves, need some kind of agreed-upon past. They can get it from scholars or they can get it from demagogues, but get it they will."[61]

Lepore has taken a stance opposing the very premise of The 1776 Project: "From wanting it to stop, conservatives began wanting history to turn back, not least by making a fetish of the nation's founding, in the form of originalism."[62] Those who fetishize the founding, she argues, in fact diminish "the American experiment," "making it . . . a daffy, reassuring bedtime story instead of a stirring, terrifying, inspiring, troubling, earth-shaking epic."[63] Although her warnings predate the publication of The 1776 Project, they seem particularly appropriate to the conservative stirrings that occasioned it. "The fate of the nation state itself appearing uncertain, nationalists, who had few proposals for the future, gained power by telling fables about the greatness of the past."[64] The needs of the American public cited by the writers of

The 1776 Project, "timeless stories and noble heroes," certainly have overtones of a bedtime story or fable intended for the very young.

While Lepore recognizes the "anguish" and "hypocrisy" in the American past, she is unwilling, for all that, to identify these as its warp and woof. Her own American history text, *These Truths*, is intended, she writes, to double as an "old-fashioned civics text," "an explanation of the origins and ends of democratic institutions"[65] at a moment when such institutions, in her view—and not only hers—are threatened.

If on the basis of a coherent history a nation can imagine a viable future, the end of Lepore's text should give us pause.

> It would fall to a new generation of Americans, reckoning what their forebears had wrought, to fathom the depths of the doom-black Sea. If they meant to repair the tattered ship, they would need to fill the most majestic pine in a deer-haunted forest and raised the new mast that could pierce the clouded sky.[66]

Some reviews of this work balk at this extended metaphor. [67] For Lepore, an historian steeped in particulars and events, this conjuring of the future, conveyed in metaphor and imagery, and in the conditional mood rather than the future tense, is an indication of how intransigently difficult it is for a nation to "account" for itself and through that accounting to lay the foundations for a future. It might also signal the difficulty of imagining a future from the vantage point of our present junction.

Susan Neiman attempts to take America's "original sin" out of the realm of the singular and incomparable. "American sins are not worse than those of other nations," she asserts, "they're simply more jarring because, unlike the foundation of other nations, America's took place amid a fanfare of ideals."[68] I think the French might also claim that the birth of their nation was heralded by a similar "fanfare of ideals," and for that reason found 1940 so particularly cataclysmic.

> There shouldn't be a single sincerely freedom-loving person in the world who could believe that there are legitimate reasons to hate France; all serious human beings who love liberty should be happy that France exists. We believe that is the case, but that's a mistake; it depends on us from this point on to make it so.[69]

Simone Weil, too, in addressing her fellow countrymen and -woman, chose the conditional mood. Her apostrophe is a recognition of France's calling, a sad admission of failure to answer that calling, an exhortation to work to assure the challenge is, in the future, met. Almost 80 years later, she speaks directly to different people on a different continent. The challenge is still there to be taken up.

NOTES

1. Robert Chenavier, "Avant-propos I," *L'Enracinement, OC* V, Vol. 2 (Paris: Gallimard, 2013), 16.
2. "Prostrée, étendue à terre, encore à demi assomée, peut-être peut-elle quand même essayer de commencer de nouveau à penser le destin du monde. Non pas en décider, car elle n'a aucune autorité pour cela. Le penser, ce qui est tout à fait différent."
   Simone Weil, "A propos de la question coloniale dans ses rapports avec le destin du peuple français," *OC* V, Vol. 1 (Paris: Gallimard, 2019), 295.
3. "plus grand justice sociale."
   "France politique. CE. Réseaux et organisations de résistance": questionnaire relatif aux pouvoirs à mettre en place à la Libération et remarques sur ce questionnaire. 1er mars 1943 Archives du Comité d'histoire de la Deuxième Guerre mondiale—Résistance intérieure: mouvements, réseaux, partis politiques et syndicats. https://www.siv.archives-nationales.culture.gouv.fr/siv/rechercheconsultation/consultation/ir/consultationIR.action?irId=FRAN_IR_053870&udId=cu00dio35v2-1k9p94vi7oyzu&details=true&gotoArchivesNums=false&auSeinIR=true.
4. Andrew Shennen, *Rethinking France: Plans for Renewal 1940–1946* (New York: Oxford University Press, 1989), 37.
5. Among other provisions, the Constitution of the Fourth Republic included the following: Political parties would produce platforms so voters would choose policy rather than personalities; the Assembly was bicameral, with the senate's power much reduced; the legislative process was reorganized to avoid the "congestion" that characterized legislation during the Third Republic; the legislature was given a larger role in regulating the economy and social programs; the executive was granted more power. Shennen, *Rethinking*, 138–39. The Constitution of the Fifth Republic would in its turn try to remedy some of the shortcomings of that of the Fourth, particularly the ineffective executive. Article 17 of the 1958 Constitution assured that France had one of the strongest heads of state in Europe, according to Julian Jackson (*The Fall of France*, 241), granted such powers that even an "honorable nonentity" (Jackson's tag) such as Albert Lebrun, the last president of the Third Republic who acquiesced to its dismantling, might have had the tools to face an emergency, according to Stanley Hoffmann. "The Trauma of 1940: A Disaster and Its Traces," in *The French Defeat of 1940: Reassessments*, ed. Joel Blatt (Providence, Berghahn Books, 1998), 367.
6. Simone Weil, *L'Enracinement, OC* V, Vol. 2 (Paris: Gallimard, 2013), 257.
7. Simone Weil, "Structure du gouvernement et création d'un parti," *OC* V, Vol. 1 (Paris: Gallimard, 2019), 440.
8. Some have characterized her support for some of these proposals and her unwillingness to reject as noxious all of Vichy's policy proposals as a collaborationist stance.
9. Shennen, *Rethinking*, 166–68.
10. Simone Weil, "À propos de la question coloniale," 281.
11. Robert Chenavier, "Présentation," *OC* V, Vol. 1 (Paris: Gallimard, 2019), 48.
12. Schumann, the spokesman for De Gaulle, was the primary voice heard in the radio program "Honneur et Patrie." As early as 1941, he encourages his listeners in

France to denounce the traitors among them by marking their houses with a "T." And he further assures his audience that lists are being drawn up and a severe punishment awaits the miscreants.

Jacques Pessis, *Les Français parlent aux Français 1941–1942* (Np: Omnibus, 2011), 151.

13. "Une justice n'est sévère que si elle est rapide."

Journal Officiel France combattante. Comité français de la libération nationale (28 août 1944) (Alger: Imprimerie officielle du gouvernement général de l'Algérie, 1944), 767. https://gallica.bnf.fr/ark:/12148/bpt6k9622107p/f3.item.

14. Pessis, *Les Français*, 1311.

15. "Mais le principe d'égalité devant la loi ne s'oppose pas à ce que la nation fasse le partage des bons et des mauvais citoyens."

Journal Officiel, 767.

16. "Je n'aime pas beaucoup entendre des gens parfaitement comfortable [*sic*] ici traiter de lâches et de traîtres ceux qui, en France, se débrouillent comme ils peuvent dans une situation terrible. Il y a un petit nombre de Français seulement pour qui il soit à peu près sûr que ces adjectifs sont mérités; on ne devrait pas les étendre au-delà. . . . On ne devrait employer le mot de traître que pour désigner ceux dont on est certain qu'ils désirent la victoire de l'Allemagne et font ce qu'ils peuvent à cet effet. Quant aux autres, certains de ceux qui acceptent de travailler avec Vichy, et même avec les Allemands, peuvent avoir des motifs honorables répondant à des situations déterminées. D'autres peuvent être l'objet de pressions telles qu'ils ne pourraient résister sans héroïsme. Or la plupart des gens qui s'érigent en juges ici n'ont jamais eu l'occasion d'éprouver s'ils sont eux-mêmes des héros."

Qtd. in Simone Pétrement, *Vie de Simone Weil* Vol. II (Paris: Fayard, 1973), 445–46.

17. "désigner le pur et l'impur dans le même mouvement, [d]'éliminer les mauvais Français mais aussi [de] recomposer une identité collective."

Pierre Truche and Denis Salas, *La Justice de l'épuration à la fin de la Second Guerre Mondiale* (Paris: la Documentation française, 2008), 18.

18. See Julian Jackson *The Fall of France: The Nazi Invasion of 1940* (New York: Oxford University Press, 2003), 192.

19. Given this lacuna, the ground was free for British and American historians to step in with such works as William Shirer's 1969 *The Collapse of the Third Republic: An Inquiry into the Fall of France 1940* and Robert Paxton's 1972 *Vichy France: Old Guard and New Order, 1940–1944*.

20. Weil, *L'Enracinement*, 198–201.

21. Henry Rousso, *The Vichy Syndrome*, trans. Arthur Goldhammer (Cambridge, MA: Harvard University Press, 1991), 11.

22. Rousso, *Vichy*, 303.

23. Rousso, *Vichy*, 50.

24. Qtd. in Rousso, *Vichy*, 123.

25. "brutalement resurgi dans la mémoire des Français."

Eric Conan and Henry Rousso, *Vichy: Un passé qui ne passe pas* (Fayard: Paris, 1994), 9.

26. "La première leçon de la psychanalyse est ici que le trauma demeure même quand il est inaccessible, indisponible. À sa place surgissent des phénomènes de substitution, des symptômes qui masquent le retour du refoulé sous de guises diverses." Paul Ricœur, *La mémoire, l'histoire, l'oubli* (Paris: Seuil, 2000), 576.

27. Stanley Hoffmann, Preface to *The Vichy Syndrome*, x.

28. Madeleine K. Albright, Interview on NBC-TV "The Today Show" with Matt Lauer Columbus, Ohio, February 19, 1998, US Dept of State Archive. https://1997-2001.state.gov/statements/1998/980219a.html.

29. Valerie Strauss, "Why Republican efforts to ban the 1619 Project from classrooms are so misguided," *Washington Post*, April 7, 2021, https://www.washingtonpost.com/education/2021/04/07/why-republican-efforts-to-ban-1619-project-classrooms-are-so-misguided/.

30. Nikole Hannah-Jones, "Introduction," *The 1619 Project*, *The New York Times Magazine*, August 18, 2019: 4–5, https://pulitzercenter.org/sites/default/files/full_issue_of_the_1619_project.pdf.

31. In a letter to the Editors of the *New York Times*, Sean Wilentz, Victoria Bynum, James McPherson, James Oakes, and Gordon S. Wood, all noted American historians, take issue at length with this assertion. *The Times* published their response as well as the original letter.

"We Respond to the Historians Who Critiqued The 1619 Project," *New York Times*, Jan. 19, 2021.

https://www.nytimes.com/2019/12/20/magazine/we-respond-to-the-historians-who-critiqued-the-1619-project.html.

32. Hannah-Jones, "Introduction," 18.

33. This assertion likewise gets pushback from Wilentz et al., who remind their readers of the white American partners who toiled alongside black Americans during Reconstruction.

34. Hannah-Jones, "Introduction," 21.

35. Hannah-Jones, "Introduction," 26.

36. Hannah-Jones, "Introduction," 16.

37. This "pessimism" as well as the focus on racial to the exclusion of class conflict are the recurring objection to the 1619 Project on The World Socialist Website and the International Committee of the Fourth International that it represents. They joined the debate vociferously and early, and the materials first published on their website were later gathered into a collection of essays.

The New York Times 1619 Project, World Socialist Website. https://www.wsws.osrg/en/topics/event/1619.

David North and Thomas Mackaman, eds., *The New York Times' 1619 Project and the Racialist Falsification of History* (Royal Oak, MI: Mehring, 2021).

38. The 1776 Report, The President's Advisory 1776 Commission, 18, https://trumpwhitehouse.archives.gov/wp-content/uploads/2021/01/The-Presidents-Advisory-1776-Commission-Final-Report.pdf.

39. The 1776 Report, 1.

40. The 1776 Report, 10.

41. The 1776 Report, 13.

42. The 1776 Report, 34.
43. The 1776 Report, 11.
44. The 1776 Report, 15.
45. The 1776 Report, 1.
46. Rousso, *Vichy*, 4.
47. Susan Nieman, *Learning from the Germans: Confronting Race and the Memory of Evil* (London: Allen Lane, 2019), 266.
48. Neiman, *Learning*, 264.
49. Neiman, *Learning*, 269.
50. Mitch Landrieu, "Speech on the Removal of Confederate Monuments in New Orleans," *The New York Times* May 23, 2017. https://www.nytimes.com/2017/05/23/opinion/mitch-landrieus-speech-transcript.html.
51. Qtd. Neiman, *Learning*, 278.
52. Landrieu, "Speech."
53. Whose Heritage: Public Symbols of the Confederacy. Southern Poverty Law Center, 2016. https://www.splcenter.org/sites/default/files/com_whose_heritage.pdf.
54. Landrieu, "Speech."
55. Simone Weil, *Cahiers, OC* VI, Vol. 1, (Paris: Gallimard, 1994), 220.
56. For background, Rashawn Ray and Alexandra Gibbons, "Why are States Banning Critical Race Theory?" *Brookings*, November 2021. https://brook.gs/3ht9RMC; Stephen Sawchuck, "What is Critical Race Theory, and Why Is It Under Attack?" *Education Week*, May 18, 2021. https://www.edweek.org/leadership/what-is-critical-race-theory-and-why-is-it-under-attack/2021/05.
57. An Act Relating to the Social Studies Curriculum in Public Schools, House Bill 3979, May 2021, Eighty-seventh Texas Legislature. https://capitol.texas.gov/tlodocs/87R/billtext/pdf/HB03979F.pdf#navpanes=0.
58. Landrieu, "Speech."
59. Neiman, *Learning*, 269.
60. Qtd. in Jill Lepore, *This America: The Case for the Nation* (New York: Liveright, 2019), 16.
61. Lepore, *This America*, 19–20.
62. Jill Lepore, *These Truths: A History of the United States*, 1st ed. (New York: W.W. Norton & Company, 2018), 787.
63. Lepore, *These Truths*, 788.
64. Lepore, *These Truths*, 788.
65. Lepore, *These Truths*, xviii.
66. Lepore, *These Truths*, 788.
67. It makes George Scialabba "wince," and he is sure it would not have gotten past one of her editors at the *New Yorker*, while John McGreevy tells his reader they might well "skip" the extended metaphor of the final sentences.

George Scialabba, "Affirming America," *Raritan* 39, no. 3 (Winter 2020): 15. https://search.ebscohost.com/login.aspx?direct=true&AuthType=cookie,ip&db=aph&AN=141857422&site=eds-live&scope=site.

John T. McGreevy, "A Noble Experiment," *Commonweal* 146, no. 1 (January 4, 2019).

https://search.ebscohost.com/login.aspx?direct=true&AuthType=cookie,ip&db=aph&AN=133574703&site=eds-live&scope=site.

68. Neiman, *Learning*, 316.

69. Simone Weil, "Reflexions en vue d'un bilan," *OC* II, Vol. 3 (Paris: Gallimard, 1989), 116.

Bibliography

The 1619 Project. *New York Times Magazine.* August 18, 2019. https://pulitzercenter.org/sites/default/files/full_issue_of_the_1619_project.pdf.
The 1776 Report. The President's Advisory 1776 Commission. https://trumpwhitehouse.archives.gov/wp-content/uploads/2021/01/The-Presidents-Advisory-1776-Commission-Final-Report.pdf.
Albright, Madeleine K., Secretary of State. Interview on NBC-TV "The Today Show" with Matt Lauer Columbus, Ohio, February 19, 1998 US Dept of State Archive. https://1997-2001.state.gov/statements/1998/980219a.html.
Amoureux, Henri. *La Grande histoire des Français sous l'occupation.* Tome I. Le peuple du désastre. 1939-40. Paris: Robert Laffont, 1976.
Andrieu, Claire. *Politiques du passé: Usages politiques du passé dans la France contemporaine*, eds. Claire Andrieu, Marie-Claire Lavabre, and Danielle Tartakowsky. Aix: Université de Provence, 2006.
Atkin, Nicholas. *Church and Schools in Vichy France, 1940–1944.* New York: Garland Pub. Inc., 1991.
Azéma, Jean-Pierre, and Michel Winock. *La IIIe République: 1870–1940.* 2nd ed. Collection Pluriel. Paris: Hachette, 1986.
Baker, Keith Michael. *Inventing the French Revolution: Essays on French Political Culture in the 18th Century.* New York: Cambridge University Press, 1990.
Beck, Julie. "Life's Stories." *The Atlantic* (August 10, 2015). https://www.theatlantic.com/health/archive/2015/08/life-stories-narrative-psychology-redemption-mental-health/400796/.
Bellescize, Diane de. "Le Comité general d'études de la Résistance." *Revue d'histoire de la Deuxième Guerre mondiale*, 25e Année, No. 99, Aspects de la Résistance française (juillet 1975): 1–24. https://www.jstor.org/stable/25728693.
Bergen, Barry H. "Primary Education in Third Republic France: Recent French Works." *History of Education Quarterly* 26, no. 2 (July 1, 1986): 271–285. doi:10.2307/368743.

Bigot, Charles. *Le Petit Français*. Paris: Eugène Weill and Georges Maurice, 1884. https://gallica.bnf.fr/ark:/12148/bpt6k948679p.

Bloch, Marc. *L'Étrange Défaite. Témoignage écrit en 1940. Suivi de Écrits clandestins 1942–44*. Paris: Albin Michel, 1957.

Blum, Léon. *A l'Echelle humaine*. In *Oeuvre de Leon Blum 1940–1945*, 407–495. Paris: Albin Michel, 1955. https://gallica.bnf.fr/ark:/12148/bpt6k20641m/f1.item.

Blum, Léon. *Devant la cour de Riom février-mars 1942*. Paris: Éditions de la liberté, 1945.

Bok, Sissela. "Simone Weil and Iris Murdoch: The Possibility of Dialogue." *Gender Issues* 22, no. 4 (Fall 2005): 71–78. doi:10.1007/s12147-005-0006-2.

Brasillach, Robert. "Comment 'les Grands Ancêtres' ont pratiqué, bien avant nos députés, la corruption parlementaire." *Je Suis Partout* 449 (June 30, 1939). https://www.retronews.fr/journal/je-suis-partout/30-juin-1939/719/2125577/1?from=%2Fsearch%23sort%3Dscore%26publishedBounds%3Dfrom%26indexedBounds%3Dfrom%26tfPublications%255B0%255D%3DJe%2520suis%2520partout%26page%3D19%26searchIn%3Dall%26total%3D683&index=449.

Brasillach, Robert. *Notre avant-guerre*. Paris: Plon, 1941.

Brueck, Katherine T. *The Redemption of Tragedy: The Literary Vision of Simone Weil*. Albany, NY: SUNY Press, 1995.

Bruhat, Jean. "La Revolution française et les masses populaires." *Cahiers du bolchévisme: organe théorique du Parti communiste français (S.F.I.C.)* July 1939: 973–991. https://gallica.bnf.fr/ark:/12148/bpt6k128314/f1.item#.

Bruner, Jerome. "The Narrative Creation of Self." In *The Handbook of Narrative and Psychotherapy: Practice, Theory and Research*, 3–14. Edited by Lynne E. Angus, John McLeod. Counseling and Psychotherapy Transcripts, Client Narratives, and Reference Works. Thousand Oaks, CA: Sage Publications, 2004. https://search-ebscohost-com.ezproxyles.flo.org/login.aspx?direct=true&AuthType=cookie,ip&db=cat05473a&AN=les.1341780&site=eds-live&scope=site.

Cabaud, Jacques. *L'experience vécue de Simone Weil*. Paris: Plon, 1957.

Chambelland, M. "La Conférence de la Pentecôte: Bloc contre la guerre et l'union sacrée." *La Révolution prolétarienne: revue mensuelle syndicaliste communiste* no. 272 (June 10, 1938): 1-169-4-172. https://gallica.bnf.fr/ark:/12148/bpt6k6289927f/f2.item.

Chenavier, Robert. "Personal Identity and National Identity: An Analogy." *Philosophical Investigations* 43, no. 1–2 (January 1, 2020): 158–164. doi:10.1111/phin.12266.

Clemenceau, Georges. "Speech before the National Assembly, Jan. 29, 1981." Great Speeches, National Assembly website https://www2.assemblee-nationale.fr/decouvrir-l-assemblee/histoire/grands-discours-parlementaires/georges-clemenceau-29-janvier-1891.

Conan, Eric and Henry Rousso. *Vichy: Un Passé qui ne passe pas. Pour une Histoire du XXe siècle*. Paris: Fayard, 1994.

Cousteau, P.-A. "La République, c'est la guerre, fraîche et joyeuse pour les lumières." *Je Suis Partout* 449 (June 30, 1939). https://www.retronews.fr/journal/je-suis-partout/30-juin-1939/719/2125577/1?from=%2Fsearch%23sort%3Dscore

%26publishedBounds%3Dfrom%26indexedBounds%3Dfrom%26tfPublications%255B0%255D%3DJe%2520suis%2520partout%26page%3D19%26searchIn%3Dall%26total%3D683&index=449.
Daladier, Edouard. "Discours le 14 juillet 1939." *Le Figaro* (July 15, 1939). https://gallica.bnf.fr/ark:/12148/bpt6k410283j/f4.item.
Dargan, Joan. *Simone Weil: Thinking Poetically*. Albany, NY: SUNY Press, 1998.
Daudet, Léon. *Les Lys sanglants: roman historique*. Paris: Flammarion, 1938.
De Gaulle, Charles. *Appels et discours 1940–1943*. N.p., 1943.
Deutsch, Karl W. "The Growth of Nations: Some Recurrent Patterns of Political and Social Integration." *World Politics* 5, no. 2 (January 1953): 168–195. doi:10.2307/2008980.
Doering, E. Jane, and Ruthann Knechel Johansen. *When Fiction and Philosophy Meet: A Conversation with Flannery O'Connor and Simone Weil*. Macon, GA: Mercer University Press, 2019.
Dunois, Amédée. "La liberté naissait: Écroulement d'un monde." *Le Populaire* No. 5992 (14 July 1939). https://www.retronews.fr/journal/le-populaire-1916-1970/14-juillet-1939/110/1191355/5.
Dupuy, Pascal. "The Revolution in History, Commemoration, and Memory." In *A Companion to the French Revolution*, 486–501. Edited by Peter McPhee. Malden, MA: John Wiley & Sons, 2013.
Fink, Carol. *Marc Bloch: A Life in History*. New York: Cambridge University Press, 1989.
Fivush, Robyn. "Speaking Silence: The Social Construction of Silence in Autobiographical and Cultural Narratives." *Memory* 18, no. 2 (February 2010): 88–98. doi:10.1080/09658210903029404.
Footit, Hilary, and John Simmonds. "Destroying the Myths of Debacle." *Durham French Studies* 3 (1991): 19–34.
Freeman, Mark Philip. *Hindsight: The Promise and Peril of Looking Backward*. New York: Oxford University Press, 2010.
Frye, Northrop. *Anatomy of Criticism*, First Princeton Paperback Edition. Princeton, NJ: Princeton University Press, 2000.
Furet, François. *Penser la Révolution française*. Nouv. éd. rev. et corr. Paris: Gallimard, 1983.
Gaxotte, Pierre. "Les deux Moteurs de la Révolution: Guerre et inflation." *Je Suis Partout* 499 (June 30, 1939). https://www.retronews.fr/journal/je-suis-partout/30-juin-1939/719/2125577/1?from=%2Fsearch%23sort%3Dscore%26publishedBounds%3Dfrom%26indexedBounds%3Dfrom%26tfPublications%255B0%255D%3DJe%2520suis%2520partout%26page%3D19%26searchIn%3Dall%26total%3D683&index=449.
Gaxotte, Pierre. "Le Personnel de la Révolution: Une Rafle à l'heure de l'apéritif." *Je Suis Partout* 447 (June 16, 1939). https://www.retronews.fr/journal/je-suis-partout/16-juin-1939/719/2125553/1?from=%2Fsearch%23sort%3Dscore%26publishedBounds%3Dfrom%26indexedBounds%3Dfrom%26tfPublications%255B0%255D%3DJe%2520suis%2520partout%26page%3D19%26searchIn%3Dall%26total%3D683&index=449.
Grillen-Ricard, I. de. "Le Peuple contre la terreur." *Je Suis Partout* 449 (June 30, 1939). https://www.retronews.fr/journal/je-suis-partout/30-juin-1939/719/2125577/1

?from=%2Fsearch%23sort%3Dscore%26publishedBounds%3Dfrom%26indexed-Bounds%3Dfrom%26tfPublications%255B0%255D%3DJe%2520suis%2520partout%26page%3D19%26searchIn%3Dall%26total%3D683&index=449.
Halbwachs, Maurice. *The Collective Memory*. 1st ed. Harper Colophon Books. New York: Harper & Row, 1980.
Halévy, Daniel. *Histoire d'une histoire*. Paris: B. Grasset, 1939.
Hannah Jones, Nikole. "Introduction" to *The 1619 Project*. *New York Times Magazine*. August 18, 2019. https://pulitzercenter.org/sites/default/files/full_issue_of_the_1619_project.pdf.
Herriot, Edouard. *Aux Sources de la liberté*. Paris: Gallimard, 1939.
Hobsbawn, Eric. "Introduction, Inventing Traditions." In *The Invention of Tradition*, 1–14. Edited by E. J. Hobsbawm and T. O. Ranger. Cambridge: Cambridge University Press, 2012.
Hoffmann, Stanley. Preface to *The Vichy Syndrome*, by Henry Rousso, vii–x. Cambridge, MA: Harvard University Press, 1991.
Hoffmann, Stanley. "The Trauma of 1940: A Disaster and Its Traces." In *The French Defeat of 1940: Reassessments*, 354–380. Edited by Joel Blatt. Providence: Berghahn Books, 1998.
L'Humanité. 15 juillet 1939. https://gallica.bnf.fr/ark:/12148/bpt6k407873r.
Hunt, Lynn. Preface to *Festivals and the French Revolution*, by Mona Ozouf, ix–xiii. Cambridge, MA: Harvard University Press, 1988.
Hutton, Patrick H. *History as an Art of Memory*. Lebanon, NH: University Press of New England, 1993.
Jackson, Julian. *The Fall of France: The Nazi Invasion of 1940*. New York: Oxford University Press, 2003.
Jaurès, Jean. "Aux Instituteurs et Institutrices." In *Action socialiste: Première série*, 15–20. Paris: Bellais, 1899. https://gallica.bnf.fr/ark:/12148/bpt6k827450/.
Jaurès, Jean. "La France et le socialism." In *Action socialiste: Première série*, 372–378. Paris: Bellais, 1899. https://gallica.bnf.fr/ark:/12148/bpt6k827450/.
Je Suis Partout. Numéro dédié à la Révolution. No. 449 (June 30, 1939). https://www.retronews.fr/journal/je-suis-partout/30-juin-1939/719/2125577/1?from=%2Fsearch%23sort%3Dscore%26publishedBounds%3Dfrom%26indexedBounds%3Dfrom%26tfPublications%255B0%255D%3DJe%2520suis%2520partout%26page%3D19%26searchIn%3Dall%26total%3D683&index=449.
Josselson, Ruthellen. "On Becoming the Narrator of One's Own Life." In *Healing Plots: The Narrative Basis of Psychotherapy*, 111–127. The Narrative Study of Lives. Washington, DC: American Psychological Association, 2004. doi:10.1037/10682-006.
Journal officiel. France combattante. Comité français de la libération nationale, 28 août 1944. Algiers: Imprimerie officielle du gouvernement général de l'Algérie. https://gallica.bnf.fr/ark:/12148/bpt6k9622107p/f3.item.
Keita, Mamadi. "Critique de l'état-nation dans '*L'Enracinement*' de Simone Weil." *CLA Journal* 46, no. 4 (June 1, 2003): 543–561. https://search-ebscohost-com.ezproxyles.flo.org/login.aspx?direct=true&AuthType=cookie,ip&db=edsjsr&AN=edsjsr.44325183&site=eds-live&scope=site.

Laborie, Pierre. *L'Opinion française sous Vichy*. Paris: Seuil, 1990.
Lackerstein, Debbie. *National Regeneration in Vichy France: Ideas and Policies, 1930–1944*. Burlington, VT: Ashgate, 2012.
Landrieu, Mitch. "Speech on the Removal of Confederate Monuments in New Orleans." *The New York Times,* May 23, 2017. https://www.nytimes.com/2017/05/23/opinion/mitch-landrieus-speech-transcript.html.
Larson, Kate. "'The Most Intimate Bond': Metaxological Thinking in Simone Weil and Iris Murdoch." In *Iris Murdoch Connected: Critical Essays on Her Fiction and Philosophy*, 155–168. Edited by Mark Luprecht. University of Tennessee Press, 2014. ProQuest Ebook Central, https://ebookcentral.proquest.com/lib/lesley/detail.action?docID=4415939.
Lavisse, Ernest. *Histoire de France: Cours élémentaire*. Paris: Armand Colin, 1913. https://gallica.bnf.fr/ark:/12148/bpt6k14213780.
Lavisse, Ernest. "Lettres ouvertes aux instituteurs de France." In *Manuel général de l'instruction primaire: journal hebdomadaire des instituteurs*. 65e année, tome 34, 85–87. Paris: Hachette, 1898. https://education.persee.fr/doc/magen_1257-5593_1898_num_65_34_32325.
Lavisse, Ernest. *Questions d'Enseignement national*. Paris: Armand Colin, 1885.
Lepore, Jill. *These Truths: A History of the United States*. First ed. New York: W.W. Norton & Company, 2018.
Lepore, Jill. *This America: The Case for the Nation*. First ed. New York: Liveright Publishing Corporation, 2019.
Louzon, Robert. "Tchécoslovaquie et France." *La Révolution prolétarienne* no. 280 (October 10, 1938): 1-305–7-311. https://gallica.bnf.fr/ark:/12148/bpt6k62899350.
Louzon, Robert. "La Question des Sudètes." *La Révolution prolétarienne* no. 278 (September 10, 1938): 5-277-6-278. https://gallica.bnf.fr/ark:/12148/bpt6k62899335.
Maingueneau, Dominique. *Les Livres d'école de la République 1870–1914: discours et idéologie*. Paris: Le Sycomore, 1979.
Mayaffre, Damon. "'Nation' et 'Patrie' dans le discours de droite à la veille de la guerre: quels signifiants pour signifier quel patriotisme?" *Cahiers de lexicologie* 76, no. 1 (2000): 133–250. hal-00553874.
McGreevy, John T. "A Noble Experiment." *Commonweal* 146, no. 1 (January 4, 2019): 24–26. https://search.ebscohost.com/login.aspx?direct=true&AuthType=cookie,ip&db=aph&AN=133574703&site=eds-live&scope=site.
McLean, Kate C., Jennifer P. Lilgendahl, Chelsea Fordham, Elizabeth Alpert, Emma Marsden, Kathryn Szymanowski, and Dan P. McAdams. "Identity Development in Cultural Context: The Role of Deviating from Master Narratives." *Journal of Personality* 86, no. 4 (August 2018): 631–651. doi:10.1111/jopy.12341.
Merlio, Gilbert. "Le Pacifisme en Allemagne et en France entre les deux guerres mondiales." *Les Cahiers Irice* 8, no. 2 (2011): 39–59. doi:10.3917/lci.008.0039.
Michon, Georges. "Comment abattre le fascism." *La Révolution prolétarienne* no. 264 (February 10, 1938): 12–44. https://gallica.bnf.fr/ark:/12148/bpt6k6289919w?rk=64378;0.
Murdoch, Iris. *The Nice and Good*. New York: Penguin, 1968.

Nelms, Brenda. *The Third Republic and the Centennial of 1889*. New York: Garland, 1987.

The New York Times 1619 Project. World Socialist Website. https://www.wsws.osrg/en/topics/event/1619.

Nieman, Susan. *Learning from the Germans: Confronting Race and the Memory of Evil*. London: Allen Lane, 2019.

North, David and Thomas Mackaman, editors. *The New York Times' 1619 Project and the Racialist Falsification of History*. Royal Oak, MI: Mehring, 2021.

Ory, Pascal. "La Commémoration révolutionnaire en 1939." In *La France et les français en 1938–1939*, 115–136. Edited by René Rémond et Janine Bourdin. Paris: Fondation nationale des sciences politiques, 1978.

Ory, Pascal. "Le Cent-cinquantenaire, ou comment s'en débarasser." In *La Légende de la Révolution au XXe siècle: De Gance à Renoir, de Romain Roland à Claude Simone*, 139–156. Edited by Jean-Claude Bonnet et Philippe Roger. Paris: Flammarion, 1988.

Ory, Pascal. *Une Nation pour memoire: 1889, 1939, 1989. Trois jubilés révolutionnaires*. Paris: Presses de la Fondation Nationale des Sciences Politiques, 1992.

Ozouf, Jacques, and Mona Ozouf. *La République des instituteurs*. Hautes études. Paris: Gallimard: Seuil, 1992.

Ozouf, Mona, and Jacques Ozouf. "Le Thème du patriotisme dans les manuels primaires." *Mouvement Social* no. 49 (Oct.–Dec. 1964): 5–31. doi:10.2307/3777137.

Ozouf, Mona. "Jules Ferry." Lecture given at conference on Jules Ferry. Bibliothèque nationale, Paris, France, April 22, 2003, videotaped lecture. https://gallica.bnf.fr/ark:/12148/bpt6k1320764s?rk=21459;2.

Ozouf, Mona. *Jules Ferry: La Liberté et la tradition*. Paris: Gallimard, 2014.

Paxton, Robert O. *Vichy France: Old Guard and New Order, 1940–1944*. New York: Knopf, 1972.

Perrin, Joseph-Marie, and Gustave Thibon. *Simone Weil telle que nous l'avons connue*. Paris: La Colombe, 1952.

Pessis, Jacques, ed. *Les Français parlent aux Français. 1941–1942*. Np: Omnibus, 2011.

Le Petit Journal. 15 juillet 1939. https://gallica.bnf.fr/ark:/12148/bpt6k636938f.

Le Petit Parisien. 15 juillet 1939. https://gallica.bnf.fr/ark:/12148/bpt6k6837305.

Pétrement, Simone. *La vie de Simone Weil: 1909–1934*. Paris: Fayard, 1973.

Pollard, David. *The Continuing Legacy of Simone Weil*. New York: Hamilton, 2015.

Le Populaire. 15 juillet 1939. https://gallica.bnf.fr/ark:/12148/bpt6k8234654/f1.image.

Propp, V. Ia., Svatava Pírková-Jakobsonová, Louis A. Wagner, and Alan Dundes. *Morphology of the Folktale*. 2d Ed., Rev. and Edited with a Pref. by Louis A. Wagner and New Introd. by Alan Dundes. ed. Publications of the American Folklore Society. Bibliographical and Special Series; v. 9. Austin: University of Texas Press, 1968.

Prost, Antoine. *Histoire de l'enseignement en France 1800–1967*. Paris: Armand Colin, 1968.

Raïd, Layla. "Iris Murdoch et Simone Weil: l'attention." In *Mélanges en l'honneur de René Daval*. Edited by Véronque Leru et Pierre Frath. EPURE. Éditions et Presses Universitaires de Reims, 2019. ⟨halshs-02976588⟩.

Rambaud, Alfred. *Jules Ferry*. Paris: Plon, 1903. https://gallica.bnf.fr/ark:/12148/bpt6k11751200?rk=21459;2.

Rebatet, Lucien. *Les Décombres*. Paris: Denoel, 1942.

Renan, Ernest. "Nouvelle Lettre à M. Strauss." In *La Reforme Intellectuelle et morale*, 3rd ed., 187–209. Paris: Michel Lévy, Frères, 1872.

Renan, Ernest. *Qu'est-ce qu'une nation?: Conférence faite en Sorbonne, le 11 mars 1882*. 2nd ed. Paris: Calmann-Lévy, 1882. https://fr.wikisource.org/wiki/Qu%E2%80%99est-ce_qu%E2%80%99une_nation_%3F.

Ricoeur, Paul. *La Mémoire, l'histoire, l'oubli*. Paris: Seuil, 2000.

Robespierre, Maximilien. "'Discours sur la guerre," prononcé à la Société des Amis de la Constitution, le 2 janvier 1792, an quatrième de la Révolution." *Discours par Maximilien Robespierre – 5 Février 1791–11 Janvier 1792*. Project Gutenberg. https://www.gutenberg.org/files/29775/29775-h/29775-h.htm.

Rodinson, Maxime. "Le Marxisme et la nation." *L'Homme et la société* 7, no. 1 (1968): 131–149.

Roland, Patrice. "Avant-propos I" to *L'Enracinement*, *OC* V, Vol. 2, by Simone Weil, 12–45. Paris: Gallimard, 2013.

Rousso, Henry. *The Vichy Syndrome*. Translated by Arthur Goldhammer. Cambridge: Harvard University Press, 1991.

Schklovsky, Viktor. *Theory of Prose*. Translated by Benjamin Sher. Elmwood Park: Dalky Archive Press, 1990.

Scialabba, George. "Affirming America." *Raritan* 39, no. 3 (Winter 2020): 15–30. https://search.ebscohost.com/login.aspx?direct=true&AuthType=cookie,ip&db=aph&AN=141857422&site=eds-live&scope=site.

Serret, Gilbert. "Tous debout contre la Guerre qui rôde." *Revue pédagogique: L'École émancipée* 21, no. 1 (2 October 1938): 3–7. https://gallica.bnf.fr/ark:/12148/bpt6k6751960z/f7.item.

Shennen, Andrew. *Rethinking France: Plans for Renewal, 1940–1946*. New York: Oxford University Press, 1989.

Siegel, Mona L. *The Moral Disarmament of France: Education, Pacifism and Patriotism, 1914–1940*. New York: Cambridge University Press, 2004.

Soboul, Albert. *1789: An I de la Liberté*. Paris: Editions Sociales Internationales, 1939.

Springsted, Eric. *Simone Weil for the Twenty-First Century*. South Bend: University of Notre Dame Press, 2021. Epub.

Stokes, Thomas. *Audience, Intention, and Rhetoric in Pascal and Simone Weil*. New York; Washington, DC; Baltimore: Peter Lang, 1996.

Strauss, Valerie. "Why Republican Efforts to Ban the 1619 Project from Classrooms are so Misguided." *Washington Post* (April 7, 2021). https://www.washingtonpost.com/education/2021/04/07/why-republican-efforts-to-ban-1619-project-classrooms-are-so-misguided/.

Thiesse, Anne-Marie. *Faire les Français: Quelle identité nationale?* Paris: Stock, 2010.

Thorez, Maurice. "Le 150e Anniversaire" (Discours à Buffalo – 26 juin 1939). *Cahiers du bolchévisme: organe théorique du Parti communiste français (S.F.I.C)* (July 1939): 899–906. https://gallica.bnf.fr/ark:/12148/bpt6k128314/f1.item#.

Thouvenin, Jean. *La France Nouvelle.* V. 1, 2, 4 and 5. Paris: Sequana, 1940.

Truche, Pierre, and Denis Salas. *La Justice de l'épuration à la fin de la Seconde Guerre Mondiale.* Paris: la Documentation française, 2008.

Tumblety, Joan. "'Civil Wars of the Mind': The Commemoration of the 1798 Revolution in the Parisian Press of The Radical Right." *European History Quarterly* 30, no. 3 (July 2000): 389–429. https://search-ebscohost-com.ezproxy-les.flo.org/login.aspx?direct=true&AuthType=cookie,ip&db=edb&AN=3435267&site=eds-live&scope=site.

"We Respond to the Historians Who Critiqued The 1619 Project." *New York Times* (January 19, 2021). https://www.nytimes.com/2019/12/20/magazine/we-respond-to-the-historians-who-critiqued-the-1619-project.html.

Weber, Eugen. *Peasants into Frenchmen: The Modernization of Rural France 1870–1914.* Stanford: Stanford University Press, 1976.

Weil, Simone. "A propos de la question coloniale dans ses rapports avec le destin du people français." In *OC* V, Vol. 1, 280–295. Paris: Gallimard, 2019.

Weil, Simone. "Allons-nous vers une révolution prolétarienne?" In *OC* II, Vol. 1, 260–281. Paris: Gallimard, 1988.

Weil, Simone. "L'Amour de Dieu et le malheur." In *OC* IV, Vol. 1, 346–374. Paris: Gallimard, 2008.

Weil, Simone. "Autobiographie spirituelle." In *Attente de Dieu,* 31–49. Edited by J.-M. Perrin. Paris: Fayard, 1966.

Weil, Simone. *Cahiers OC* VI, Vol. 1. Paris: Gallimard, 1994.

Weil, Simone. "Le centenaire de Paul Bert." *OC* II, Vol. 1, 233–235. Paris: Gallimard, 1988.

Weil, Simone. *L'Enracinement. OC* V, Vol. 2. Paris: Gallimard, 2013.

Weil, Simone. "L'Europe en guerre pour la Tchécoslovaquie?" In *OC* II, Vol. 3, 81–86. Paris: Gallimard, 1989.

Weil, Simone. "Formes de l'amour implicite de Dieu." In *OC* IV, Vol. 1, 285–336. Paris: Gallimard, 2008.

Weil, Simone. "Légitimité du gouvernement provisoire." In *OC* V, Vol. 1, 383–395. Paris: Gallimard, 2019.

Weil, Simone Weil. "La Personne et le sacré." In *OC* V, Vol. 1, 203–236. Paris: Gallimard, 2019.

Weil, Simone. "Mise au point." In *OC* II, Vol. 3, 95–98. Paris: Gallimard, 1989.

Weil, Simone. "Quelques réflexions sur les origines de l'hitlérisme." In *OC* II, Vol. 3, 168–219. Paris: Gallimard, 1989.

Weil, Simone. "Réflexions en vue d'un bilan." In *OC* II, Vol. 3, 99–116. Paris: Gallimard, 1989.

Weil, Simone. "Réflexions sans order sur l'amour de Dieu." In *OC* IV, Vol. 1, 272–279. Paris: Gallimard, 2008.

Weil, Simone. "Réflexions sur la guerre." In *OC* II, Vol. 1, 288–299. Paris: Gallimard, 1988.

White, Hayden V. *Content of the Form. Narrative Discourse and Historical Imagination.* Baltimore: Johns Hopkins University Press, 1987. 2nd printing 1989.
White, Hayden V. *Figural Realism: Studies in the Mimesis Effect.* Baltimore: Johns Hopkins University Press, 1999.
White, Hayden V. "Historical Emplotment and the Problem of Truth in Historical Representation." In *Figural Realism: Studies in the Mimesis Effect*, 27–42. Baltimore: Johns Hopkins University Press, 1999.
White, Hayden V. "Literary Theory and Historical Writing." In *Figural Realism: Studies in the Mimesis Effect*, 1–26. Baltimore: Johns Hopkins University Press, 1999.
White, Hayden V. *Metahistory: The Historical Imagination in Nineteenth-Century Europe.* Baltimore: Johns Hopkins University Press, 1973.
White, Michael. "Folk Psychology and Narrative Practice." In *The Handbook of Narrative and Psychotherapy: Practice, Theory and Research*, 22–58. Edited by Lynne E. Angus and John McLeod. Thousand Oaks, CA: Sage Publications, 2004. https://search.alexanderstreet.com/view/work/bibliographic_entity%7Cdocument%7C4722013.
Whose Heritage: Public Symbols of the Confederacy. Southern Poverty Law Center, 2016. https://www.splcenter.org/sites/default/files/com_whose_heritage.pdf.
Wright, Gordon. *Rural Revolution in France: The Peasantry in the Twentieth Century.* Stanford: Stanford University Press, 1964.
Zaretsky, Robert. *The Subversive Simone Weil: A Life in Five Ideas.* Chicago: University of Chicago Press, 2021. doi:7208/chicago/978022659477.001.0001.

Index

1619 Project, 93–94, 97–98
1776 Project, 94–95, 98–99

affliction (*malheur*), xii, xiii, 77
Alain (Émile Chartier), viii, 28
Albright, Madeleine, 92
Alliance républicaine démocrate (Republican Democratic Alliance), 28
"Allons-nous vers une révolution prolétarienne?" ("Are We Headed for a Proletarian Revolution?"), x
"L'Amour de Dieu et le malheur" ("The Love of God and Affliction"), xii, 77
Amouroux, Henri, 56, 60
Ancien Régime, 2, 12
Antigone, 16
Attente de Dieu (*Waiting for God*), xvi
attention, xii, xiii, xiv
Azéma, Jean-Pierre and Michel Winock, 2, 10, 12, 45

Bastille Day (also 14th of July), 12, 33, 36, 43
Bert, Paul, 14, 30, 31
Besseige and Lyonnais (*Histoire de France*), 32
Béziers, 18, 76, 77

Biden, Joseph, 94
Bigot, Charles, 14, 20, 31
Bloch, Marc, 57, 60–67, 79n4, 82n47
Blum, Léon, vii, ix, 28, 29, 40, 57, 59–60, 63–67, 79n4, 81n34, 82n47
Boulanger, Georges Ernest, 37, 66, 70
Brasillach, Robert, vii, 38, 39, 57, 69
Brueck, Katherine, xiii
Bynum, Victoria, 102n31

Cabaud, Jacques, xviiin3
Cabaud-Meaney, Marie, xiii
Cahiers du Bolchévisme (*Notebooks of Bolshevism*), 41
Cahiers du Sud (*Notebooks of the South*), xi, xvi
Camus, Albert, x
Carswell, Richard, 82n47
Cathars, 18, 76, 77
Catholic Church, xiii, xviin3, 1, 2, 9, 10, 18, 27, 36, 58, 67, 68, 88
Centcinquantenaire, 150th celebration of French Revolution 1939, xvi, 27, 35–47, 68, 96
Chenavier, Robert, xii, xvii
Clémenceau, Georges, 38, 42, 65, 66
collaboration, viii, 55, 58, 63, 66, 91

Collaboration Franco-allemande, Groupe (Group for French-German Collaboration), 58
Comité Générale d'Études (CGE) (General Committee for Studies), ix, 71, 88
Commemorations, historical, xvi, 17, 19, 27, 35, 37, 38, 41, 42, 47, 95, 96. *See also Centcinquantenaire*
Communist Party/communist (*Parti communiste français*), 28–30, 34, 41, 87, 88, 92
Conan, Eric, and Henry Rousso, 91
Confédération générale du travail (CGT) (General Confederation of Labor), x, 28
Constitution of 1946, 84n65, 100n5
Constitution of 1958, 100n5
Corday, Charlotte, 69
Counter-Revolution, 9, 34, 37, 45, 69
Critical Race Theory (CRT), 97
La Critique sociale (Social Critique), 31
Cult of the Lost Cause, 96

Daladier, Edouard, 29, 39, 41–43, 63
Danton, Georges, 39, 66, 68, 69
Dargan, Joan, xiii
Daudet, Leon, 69, 70
Debacle, vii, viii, xv, 21, 33, 46, 47, 55, 56, 58–61, 67, 73, 74, 77, 79n4, 82n47, 88
la Déclaration des droits de l'homme et du citoyen (Declaration of the Rights of Man and of the Citizen), 66, 71, 72, 84n64, 84n65
décréation (decreation), xiv
de Gaulle, Charles, vii, 57, 65–67, 74, 89
Deutsch, Karl W., 35
Doering, E. Jane, and Ruthanne Knechel Johansen, xiv
la drôle de guerre (the phony war), 55
Dupuy, Pascal, 10

l'École Normale Supérieure (ENS), viii, ix, 11, 28, 70

Eliot, T. S., x
L'Enracinement (The Need for Roots), ix, x, xii, xv, 46, 57, 71–78
Entre nous, xvi
l'Épuration (legal purge), 89, 90
"L'Europe en guerre pour la Tchécoslovaquie" ("Europe at War for Czechoslovakia"), 34

February 6, 1934 uprising, 69, 92
Ferry, Jules, 9, 10, 14, 16, 23n36, 30
Feuilles libres de la quinzaine (Free Sheets of the Fortnight), 34
la *Fête de la Fédération* (Festival of Federation), 43, 62
Fink, Carol, 63
Fivush, Robyn, 19, 75
Flandin, Étienne, 28, 29, 47n6
formalist literary theory, 3, 4, 6, 93
Fourth Republic, 84n65, 88, 100n5
la France combattante, la France libre (Fighting France, Free France), viii, ix, xv, 71, 84n65, 87–89
Franco-Prussian War, 1, 14, 15, 27, 33, 60, 65, 66
Freeman, Mark, 7
le Front Populaire (Popular Front), 28, 29, 41, 59, 62, 64
Frye, Northrop, 4, 6
Furet, François, 38

Gaxotte, Pierre, 38–39
Grande École, viii
grands ancêtres (French founders), 34–36, 39, 42, 44, 68, 69
Griffin, Gabrielle, xiv

Halbwachs, Maurice, 7, 35, 36
Halévy, Daniel, 39–40, 68
Hannah-Jones, Nikole, 93, 94
Herriot, Edouard, 42–45
Hitler, Adolph, x, 20, 29, 45, 55, 74
Hobsbawm, Eric, 17
Hoffmann, Stanley, 53n83, 79n4, 82n44, 91, 100n5
L'Humanité (Communist daily), 43

Index

"L'Iliade, ou le poème de la force" ("The Iliad, or the Poem of Force"), xi

indignité nationale (national indignity), 89

Jackson, Julian, 100n5
Jaurès, Jean, ix, 11, 13, 32
Je Suis Partout, 38, 39, 43, 69
Joan of Arc, 13, 62, 65, 66, 76, 77
Josselson, Ruthellen, 21

Keita, Mamadi, 84n66

Landrieu, Mitch, 95–97
Larson, Kate, xiv
Lavisse, Ernest, 11–17, 20, 24n40, 31
Lebrun, Albert, 100n5
Lepore, Jill, 98–99
life scripts, 6, 8, 13
Ligue internationale des combattants de la paix (*LICP*) (International League of Fighters for Peace), 33
Louis XIV, 13, 44, 65, 69, 74
Louis Napoleon (Napoleon III), 1, 9, 42, 65
Louzon, Robert, 33
Lycée Henri IV, viii, 28

Maingueneau, Dominique, 15
la Marseillaise, 36
Marseille, xi, xviin3, 36
Marx, Karl, and Marxism, x, 30
master narrative, xv, xvi, 3, 5–8, 11, 12, 27, 28, 56, 64; Weil's views on, 18-21. *See also* life script
Mayaffre, Damon, 28–29
McGreevy, John T., 103n67
McPherson, James, 102n31
Merleau-Ponty, Maurice, ix
Metaxu (bridge or intermediary), xiv, 76–77
Michon, Georges, 34
milieu vital (vital medium), xiii, 76–77

"Mise au point" ("A Closer Examination"), 28
Montoire summit, 55
monuments, commemorative, 17, 95–97
Mouvement républicaine populaire (MRP), 88
Munich Agreement, viii, x, 29, 30, 47n6
Murdoch, Iris, x, xii, xiii, xiv

Napoleon, 1, 13, 21n2, 42, 44, 45, 65, 76
narrative psychology, xv, 3, 6, 8, 12, 19
National Union of Teachers, 28, 30, 31
necessity, xii, 77–78
Neiman, Susan, 75, 95, 99
Nelms, Brenda, 37

Oakes, James, 102n31
obligations, xii, 71, 84n65, 84n66
Oppression and Liberty, x, 30
Ory, Pascal, 69
oubli judiciare (legal oblivion), 91
Ozouf, Jacques, 10, 12, 32
Ozouf, Mona, 1, 10, 12, 32, 36

pacifism (between the two world wars), viii, x, xvi, xviin2, 27, 28, 31–35, 51n83, 46, 61
Pantheon, 17
Paxton, Robert, 83n50
Perrin, Father Joseph-Marie, xi, xii, xvi, xviin3
"La Personne et le sacré" ("Human Personality"), xi
La Pesanteur et la grâce (Gravity and Grace), xi, xiii
Pétain, Philippe, Marshall, 1, 55, 57–59, 63, 65, 81n34, 89
Le Petit Parisien (daily), 43
Pétrement, Simone, xviin3
Plato, xiv
Le Populaire (socialist daily), 40, 43
Positivism, 9, 14, 16
la Préparation militaire supérieure (PMS), 28

Proletarian Revolution: The Emancipated School, x, 28, 31, 33, 34
Propp, Vladimir, 3–4
Prost, Antoine, 10, 14, 33

"Quelques réflexions sur les origines de l'hitlérisme" ("The Great Beast: Reflections on the Origins of Hitlerism"), xi, 44
Qu'est-ce qu'une nation? (*What is a Nation?*), 15–19

Radical Party (*Parti radical*), xvi, 19, 29, 45
Radio Londres (Radio London), 89, 100n12
Raïd, Layla, xiv
Rambaud, Alfred, 9, 23n36
Rebatet, Lucien, 38, 58, 69, 70
Reconstruction, 93–96, 102n33
"Réflexions en vue d'un bilan" ("Reflections in View of an Assessment"), xi, 44
"Réflexions sur la guerre" ("Reflections on the War"), 34
Réflexions sur les causes de la liberté et de l'oppression sociale. See Oppression and Liberty
Renan, Ernest, 15–20
Republic, First (1792), 1, 36
Republic, Second (1848), 1, 9, 36
Republic, Third (1871)
    attacks on it from Left, 40–42
    attacks on it from Right, 38–40, 58–59
    commemorations and festivals of, 12, 36
    fall of, vii, 1, 55
    Revolution as key to legitimacy of, vii, 11–14, 35, 36, 38
    "sacred history" of, vii, viii, xv–xvi, 2–3, 6, 12–14, 35, 56, 64, 65
    schooling as central to, 8–11
    Weil's critique of, 18–20, 44, 46, 73, 88

Republic, Fifth (1958), 100n5
Republic, Fourth (1946), 84n65, 88, 100n5
Resistance (French), ix, 17, 60, 72, 87, 88, 91
revanchisme (military revenge after Franco-Prussian War), 14, 27, 32, 37
revenge patriotism (after World War I), 32, 34
Revolution of 1789, xvi, 2, 10, 11, 14, 15, 17, 29
    Pacifism at its core, 34–35
    Weil's critique of, 18. *See also* Third Republic, Revolution as key to legitimacy of; *Centcinquantenaire*, 150th celebration of French Revolution
Revolution of 1848, 1
Révolution nationale. See Vichy
La Révolution prolétarienne: L'École émancipée. See The Proletarian Revolution: The Emancipated School
Richelieu, Armand Jean du Plessis, Cardinal, 44–45, 65, 74, 76
Ricoeur, Paul, 18, 20, 91
Riom trials, 59, 63–65
Robespierre, Maximilien, 34–35, 68, 69
Rodinson, Maxime, 30
Rolland, Patrice, xvii
Rome, xi
Rousso, Henry, 14, 91, 95

Saboul, Albert, 40–41
Sartre, Jean-Paul, ix
Schklovsky, Viktor, 3–4
Schumann, Maurice, 70, 89, 100n12
Scialabba, George, 103n67
Shennen, Andrew, 100n5
Shirer, William, 101n19
Siegel, Mona, 32
Socialist Party (French) (*Parti socialiste français*), 11, 13, 28, 32, 40, 59, 88, 92

Index

Southern Poverty Law Center, 96
Souvarine, Boris, 31
Springsted, Eric, xv
Stokes, Thomas, xiii
Strauss, Friedrich, 15
Syndicat national des instituteurs et des institutrices. See National Union of Teachers

Tardieu, André, 28, 29
Texas House Bill 3979, 97
Thibon, Gustave, xi, xiii, xviin3
Thiesse, Anne-Marie, vii, 17
Thorez, Maurice, 28
Trump, Donald, 92, 93, 94
Tumblety, Joan, 38, 50n48

l'Union française, 89

la Vendée, Vendéens, 69
Vichy, 55–59, 63, 65–67, 71, 72, 81n34, 87, 89
 post-war trials of members of regime, viii, 89–90
 Révolution nationale agenda, ix, 67–68, 82n49, 83n50
Vichy Syndrome, 91, 95, 97, 98

Wampole, Christy, 78
Weber, Eugen, vii, 8, 10
Weil, André (brother), viii, ix
Weil, Bernard (father), viii, ix
Weil, Selma (mother), viii, ix
Weil, Simone
 biographical sketch of, viii–x
 colonial question, 46, 71, 88–89
 death of, x, 87
 pacifism, viii, x, 10, 27–28, 31, 33, 34, 46
 patriotism, xi, 27, 31, 70, 76
 views on plans for post-war justice, 90
 works, thought of, x–xiii. *See also* Revolution of 1789, Weil's critiques of; Third Republic, Weil's critiques of
Weiland, Jean, 58–59
White, Hayden, 4–6
White, Michael, 6
Wilentz, Sean, 102n31
Wood, Gordon S., 102n31
World Socialist Website, 102n37
World War I, 11, 15, 27, 29, 31–33, 55, 60, 61, 65, 66, 73
World War II, viii, 17, 46, 55–56
Wright, Gordon, 83n50

About the Author

Christine Ann Evans is professor emerita of Comparative Literature at Lesley University, where she served as faculty and administrator. She holds a PhD from Harvard University, MAs from Harvard and Stanford University, and a BA from Stanford University. She is the author of articles on French literature, France during World War II and narrative theory.

www.ingramcontent.com/pod-product-compliance
Lightning Source LLC
Chambersburg PA
CBHW020127010526
44115CB00008B/1008